Cambridge Elements ≡

Elements in Organization Theory
edited by
Nelson Phillips
Imperial College London
Royston Greenwood
University of Alberta

COMPREHENDING THE INCOMPREHENSIBLE

Organization Theory and Child Sexual Abuse in Organizations

Donald Palmer
University of California, Davis

Valerie Feldman
University of California, Davis

CAMBRIDGE
UNIVERSITY PRESS

CAMBRIDGE
UNIVERSITY PRESS

University Printing House, Cambridge CB2 8BS, United Kingdom

One Liberty Plaza, 20th Floor, New York, NY 10006, USA

477 Williamstown Road, Port Melbourne, VIC 3207, Australia

314–321, 3rd Floor, Plot 3, Splendor Forum, Jasola District Centre, New Delhi – 110025, India

79 Anson Road, #06–04/06, Singapore 079906

Cambridge University Press is part of the University of Cambridge.

It furthers the University's mission by disseminating knowledge in the pursuit of education, learning, and research at the highest international levels of excellence.

www.cambridge.org
Information on this title: www.cambridge.org/9781108439299
DOI: 10.1017/9781108539524

First published 2018

A catalogue record for this publication is available from the British Library.

ISBN 978-1-108-43929-9 Paperback
ISSN 2397-947X (online)
ISSN 2514-3859 (print)

Comprehending the Incomprehensible

Organization Theory and Child Sexual Abuse in Organizations

Elements in Organization Theory

DOI: 10.1017/9781108539524
First published online: July 2018

Donald Palmer
University of California, Davis

Valerie Feldman
University of California, Davis

Abstract: This Element describes child sexual abuse and the formal organizations in which it can occur, reviews extant perspectives on child abuse, and explains how an organization theory approach can advance understanding of this phenomenon. It then elaborates the main paths through which organizational structures can influence child sexual abuse in organizations and analyzes how these structures operate through these paths to impact the perpetration, detection, and response to abuse. The analysis is illustrated throughout with reports of child sexual abuse published in a variety of sources. The Element concludes with a brief discussion of the policy implications of this analysis.

Keywords: organization theory, child sexual abuse,

Isbns: 9781108439299 (PB) 9781108539524 (OC)
Issns: 2397-947X (online) 2514-3859 (print)

Contents

1 Introduction

1.1 The Incomprehensible

Dr. Larry Nassar was a professor in the College of Human Medicine at Michigan State University (MSU), the official physician of the MSU gymnastics team, and a practitioner in the MSU sports medicine clinic where he treated young athletes from around the region. He also volunteered with USA Gymnastics, where he cared for US gymnasts over the course of four Olympic campaigns. In these capacities, he earned a national reputation as a devoted and skilled sports medicine physician. So much so that when corresponding with a high school athlete she was recruiting, MSU gymnastic coach Kathie Klages wrote, "We have Larry Nassar! Enough said about that!" (Hobson 2017).

Dr. Nassar was the subject of two sexual abuse allegations in 1997, the year he joined MSU. He was the subject of additional allegations in the early 2000s, again in 2004, and then again in 2014. In none of these instances was Dr. Nassar charged with sexual assault or a crime of any kind. Despite these allegations (and several associated investigations), Nassar enjoyed the support of the MSU medical school dean, his university colleagues, and the school's gymnastics coach.

It was not until September 2016 that Dr. Nassar was held accountable for his alleged misbehavior. That month another allegation of sexual assault surfaced, involving a fifteen-year-old girl. After a local newspaper reported the allegation, two women came forward claiming that Nassar had abused them as well when they were children. Another investigation was conducted, this time culminating in Nassar's firing from MSU. In November of 2016, Michigan authorities arrested Dr. Nassar on charges of sexually abusing a child. In December, federal authorities indicted him for child pornography.

For twenty-one years, Dr. Nassar had apparently been abusing girls and young women during treatment for various sports-related injuries. Further, he had accumulated "more than 37,000 (child pornographic) images and videos, including video from a Go Pro camera that showed Nassar molesting girls in a pool" (Hobson 2017). As of this time, Dr. Nassar has been convicted of three counts of child pornography, for which he has been sentenced to sixty years in prison. And he has pleaded guilty to seven counts of sexual assault, for which he will be sentenced to at least an additional forty years. In addition, over 140 women have filed civil suits against Nassar (Hobson 2017; Hobson and Rich 2017).

How can people sexually abuse children in organizations, even those devoted to caring for children? Moreover, how can people who sexually abuse children in organizations avoid detection for long periods of time, and when exposed for their abuse, escape significant punishment, again, even in organizations devoted to caring for children? When people sexually abuse children in organizations, when their abuse goes undetected, and when abusers escape meaningful punishment, it is often considered incomprehensible. Yet, systematic efforts to uncover instances of child sexual abuse in organizations suggest that these occurrences are common. An IndyStar–USA Today Network review of police files and court cases found that at least 368 US gymnasts alleged some form of sexual abuse in the past twenty years, a rate of one every twenty days (Evans, Alesia, and Kwiatkowski 2016). A *Washington Post* review of a wide range of sources found that more than 200 coaches and officials associated with US Olympic sports have been publically accused of sexual misconduct since 1982, a rate of one every six weeks (Hobson and Rich 2017). Reports from Australia (Middleton et al. 2014), as well as reports on recent child abuse scandals in the United States (Krakauer 2015), the United Kingdom (Bennhold 2016), and the Catholic Church around the world (Terry 2015), attest to the fact that child sexual abuse is a prevalent global phenomenon.

We seek to deepen understanding of these incomprehensible yet common occurrences. Specifically, we tap modern organization theory to enhance understanding of the perpetration, detection, and response to child sexual abuse in organizational contexts. In the process, we hope to contribute to organization theory, particularly that branch of theory that apprehends misconduct by and in organizations. Before beginning our pursuit of these objectives, though, we formally set the stage for our analysis. First, we define what we mean by child sexual abuse in organizational contexts. Second, we explain why we believe child sexual abuse in organizations is a topic well worth investigation. Third, we briefly review past theory and research on child sexual abuse. Finally, we indicate how our analysis will go beyond this past work and present an outline of the Element.[1]

1.2   What Is Child Sexual Abuse in Organizational Contexts?

Together, two influential definitions of child sexual abuse feature the key elements of most definitions of abuse, and provide the basis of our analysis. The World Health Organization defines child sexual abuse as:

> The involvement of a child in sexual activity that he or she does not fully comprehend, is unable to give informed consent to, or for which the child is

---

[1] This Element builds on an earlier report prepared for the Australian Royal Commission into Institutional Responses to Child Sexual Abuse (Palmer, Feldman, and McKibbin 2016).

not developmentally prepared, or else that violates the laws or social taboos of society. Children can be sexually abused by both adults and other children who are – by virtue of their age or stage of development – in a position of responsibility, trust or power over the victim

(World Health Organization 2006:10).

The Australian Royal Commission into Institutional Responses to Child Sexual Abuse defines child sexual abuse as:

> Any act that exposes a child to, or involves a child in, sexual processes beyond his or her understanding or contrary to accepted standards. Sexually abusive behaviours can include the fondling of genitals, masturbation, oral sex, vaginal or anal penetration by a penis, finger or any other object, fondling of breasts, voyeurism, exhibitionism and exposing the child to or involving the child in pornography (Bromfield 2005). It includes child grooming which refers to actions deliberately undertaken with the aim of befriending and establishing an emotional connection with a child to lower the child's inhibitions in preparation for sexual activity with the child
>
> (Royal Commission 2015:13).

Together, these definitions indicate that child sexual abuse is sexual activity involving a child that violates laws or social norms. These definitions also imply that sexual activity involving a child is abusive not just in the absence of consent (as is the case when a child is raped), but even when a child appears to offer consent, because children cannot provide *informed* consent to sexual activity. Further, these definitions imply that children cannot provide informed consent to sexual activity because they lack understanding of the meaning and implications of their involvement in such activity. Indeed, legal and normative prohibitions against children's involvement in sexual activity are rooted in the assumption that children cannot provide informed consent for this reason.

Finally, these definitions of child sexual abuse allow that perpetrators of child sexual abuse may be adults *or* children. To simplify exposition here, we distinguish between two broad categories of child sexual abuse. Instances in which the perpetrator is a legal adult and the victim a legal minor (such as the case involving Dr. Nassar described earlier) are referred to as "adult–child abuse." Instances in which both the perpetrator and victim are legal minors are referred to as "peer abuse." Adult–child abuse is the principal focus of the literature on child sexual abuse, but peer abuse is as pervasive (if not more pervasive) than adult–child abuse in organizational contexts. An international review of child sexual abuse in residential care settings found that the perpetrator was the victim's age-peer in almost one-half of reported cases (Timmerman and Schreuder 2014). This estimate roughly corresponds to Australian data covering a wide range of organizational settings (Bromfield et al. 2017), which indicate that between 62 percent and 89 percent of all *allegations* of abuse occurring in organizational contexts reported to police in Tasmania, Western Australia, and the Northern Territories involved a perpetrator under the age of eighteen, and that between 67 percent and 93 percent of all *alleged perpetrators* of abuse occurring in organizational contexts reported to police in Queensland, New South Wales, and Victoria were under the age of eighteen.[2]

The organizational contexts considered in this Element are formal organizations that incorporate children among their members. Formal organizations are collections of people engaged in sustained social interaction governed by at least a rudimentary horizontal and vertical division of labor into quasi-independent subunits, and a set of integrative mechanisms that coordinate activity across and within these subunits. Formal organizations that incorporate children include organizations whose primary purpose is caring for children (e.g., schools, sports clubs, juvenile detention centers, and foster homes) and those whose primary purpose is tangential to caring for children (e.g., religious organizations). For simplicity, we refer to both types of organizations here as "youth-serving organizations."

1.3   Why Study Child Sexual Abuse in Organizational Contexts?

Child sexual abuse is a significant social problem in most contemporary societies. It is a behavior that is prevalent, violates ethical principles, breaches social norms, breaks laws, and harms its victims (Finkelhor 1984). Child sexual abuse becomes a form of organizational wrongdoing when it occurs in organizational contexts. Individuals who abuse children violate organizational rules as well as ethical principles, social norms, and laws. Further, organizations that fail to prevent child sexual abuse or fail to promptly detect and effectively respond to abuse risk reputation loss, civil suits, and criminal liability. Hence, not only has Dr. Nassar been held accountable for his sexual assaults on young gymnasts but both MSU and USA Gymnastics are currently the target of over hundred civil suits filed on behalf of his victims (Hobson and Rich 2017).

Global meta-analyses estimate that 20 percent of girls and 8 percent of boys are sexually abused before the age of eighteen (Pereda et al. 2009; Stoltenborgh et al. 2011). Rates of abuse vary considerably cross-nationally, being higher in

---

[2] The literature on child sexual abuse often distinguishes between children and adolescents, who are sometimes referred to as "young people." For the most part, we eschew this distinction because it does not factor into our theorization of child sexual abuse in organizations. Thus, in the interests of streamlining our presentation, we refer to all perpetrators and victims of sexual abuse who are legal minors as "children."

low- and middle-income countries (CDC 2012). Australian studies estimate that up to 26 percent of girls and 16 percent of boys experience sexual abuse at some point in their childhood (Price-Robertson, Bromfield, and Vassallo 2010). Research reveals a strong link between child sexual abuse and a range of short- and long-term adverse health consequences. Victims are more likely than non-victims to experience poor mental health, including depression and posttraumatic stress disorder (Paolucci, Genuis, and Violato 2001), attempt and commit suicide (Cashmore and Shackel 2013). They also are more likely to report problems developing secure, healthy attachments with others (Whiffen and MacIntosh 2005) and abuse alcohol (Cutajar et al. 2010), be convicted of a criminal offence, or become the victim of a crime (Ogloff et al. 2012).

While the majority of child sexual abuse occurs in the home or community (Richards 2011; Stoltenborgh et al. 2011), a significant amount occurs in youth-serving organizations. There are no comprehensive large-scale studies on the frequency of child sexual abuse across the full range of youth-serving organizations. However, one study found that 10.3 percent of children living in youth justice centers reported sexual abuse at the hands of a staff member during their incarceration (Beck, Harrison, and Guerino 2010). Another found that 9.6 percent of public school students in the United States reported sexual abuse perpetrated by an educator while in school (Shakeshaft 2004). While researchers differ on whether child sexual abuse is more prevalent in organizations, as opposed to community and family contexts (Euser et al. 2013; Schumacher and Carlson 1999), most agree that child sexual abuse in organizations is qualitatively different than abuse in other settings, as it is more likely to involve multiple perpetrators (Schumacher and Carlson 1999) who abuse multiple victims (Richards 2011).

1.4   Previous Analyses of Child Sexual Abuse

Three disciplines currently dominate the analysis of child sexual abuse: criminology, public health, and social work. Criminologists predominantly are motivated by the desire to thwart and apprehend perpetrators of child sexual abuse, because abuse is considered a crime. Thus, they primarily focus on identifying the conditions associated with abuse and characterizing the modus operandi used by perpetrators of abuse. Because criminologists tend to assume that persons who perpetrate abuse are rational actors, they concentrate on identifying conditions that provide perpetrators with the opportunity to abuse children undetected. Further, they seek to ascertain the strategies that perpetrators use to lay the foundation for abuse, referred to as "grooming" and discussed in detail in the following (cf. Clark 2008).

Public health researchers are largely motivated by the desire to eradicate child sexual abuse, insofar as abuse is considered injurious to public health. Thus, they too tend to focus on identifying the conditions associated with abuse. But because public health scholars are not constrained by a particular model of human behavior, rational or otherwise, they tend to search for a wider range of conditions that are associated with abuse. Specifically, they tend to conduct large sample quantitative empirical analyses in which they seek to identify "risk factors" that are correlated with the occurrence of abuse, typically offering only post hoc speculations about the mechanisms that might generate the empirical associations (cf. Letourneau et al. 2014; Letourneau 2016).

Social work scholars are motivated by the desire to protect children from sexual abuse, because abuse is known to have significant harmful consequences for children. Thus, like criminologists, social work scholars focus on both identifying the conditions associated with abuse and characterizing the modus operandi employed by perpetrators of abuse. In pursuit of these objectives, they tend to borrow from and build on the work of both criminologists and public health scholars described earlier (cf. Keenan 2012).

A small number of sociologists also have analyzed child sexual abuse. Sociologists do not have a professional obligation to thwart and apprehend perpetrators of abuse, eradicate the social pathology of abuse, or protect children from abuse. Rather, they are, for better and worse, free to pursue an understanding of child sexual abuse as a social phenomenon, often in conjunction with elaborating and testing a favored theoretical perspective. While sociologists constitute a small minority of scholars who analyze child sexual abuse, one sociologist, David Finkelhor (1984) has produced a theory of the preconditions of abuse that has been widely embraced by those working in the fields of criminology, public health, and social work and that we discuss in detail in the following.[3]

While extremely important, prior analyses of child sexual abuse suffer from two limitations when applied to child sexual abuse in organizational contexts. First, theorization of the process by which instances of child sexual abuse unfold has been limited by the implicit assumption that in all instances perpetrators are rational actors who intentionally "groom" their victims for abuse. Second, theorization of the causes, detection, and response to child sexual abuse in organizations fails to take into account the formal organizational context in which children can be abused. Psychologists and sociologists

---

[3] Each of these disciplines as well as the fields of psychology and psychiatry (cf., Herman 2015) also develops theory and conduct research on the treatment of victims and, to a lesser extent, the perpetrators of child sexual abuse. We do not discuss this work here, because it is tangential to the focus of our analysis.

understand formal organizations to be "strong situations," in that they consist of structures that can override individual predispositions and shape member attitudes and behavior (Pfeffer and Davis-Blake 1989). Here, we offer an expanded analysis of child sexual abuse in organizational contexts that directly addresses these prior limitations.

1.5 Plan of the Element

In this Element we develop a more comprehensive theorization of the process through which instances of child sexual abuse can unfold in organizations, which allows that perpetrators may sometimes enact abusive relationships with children in a less than fully rational and premeditated manner. We also tap contemporary organization theory to analyze how five key organizational structures influence the unfolding of, detection, and response to child sexual abuse in organizations.

We begin by building on Finkelhor's pathbreaking sociological analysis of the preconditions of child sexual abuse to delineate the principal paths through which organizational structures can influence child sexual abuse (Section 2). We then discuss five organizational structures that we believe can influence the perpetration, detection, and response to abuse. The first two structures – incentive systems and administrative systems – have received relatively comprehensive attention in prior work and thus are considered together only briefly (Section 3). The following three structures – power configurations, cultural arrangements, and institutional structures – have received less adequate attention and thus are discussed at greater length in Sections 4, 5, and 6. We then consider a unique form of formal organization that we believe is particularly problematic from the standpoint of the perpetration, detection, and response to abuse: total institutions (Section 7). In the final section, we consider the implications of our analysis for practitioners and organizational theorists.

Throughout the Element, we illustrate our analysis with descriptions of actual instances of child sexual abuse in organizations from reports in a wide variety of newspapers, news magazines, and books from around the globe. We make extensive reference, however, to instances of abuse that occurred in Australia over the last forty-fifty years, described in case studies prepared by the Australian Royal Commission into Institutional Responses to Child Sexual Abuse (Appendix I). When referencing these instances of abuse, three-letter identifiers created by the Royal Commission to preserve the anonymity of abuse survivors and alleged perpetrators are usually used to refer to victims and perpetrators of abuse.

2 The Paths through Which Organizational Structures Can Influence Child Sexual Abuse in Organizations

2.1 Finkelhor's Four Preconditions Model

Finkelhor's (1984) highly influential model of the factors leading perpetrators to abuse children across multiple settings provides our basis for specifying paths through which organizational structures influence the perpetration of child sexual abuse in organizations. Finkelhor identifies four preconditions: (1) perpetrators must possess motivation to abuse children or a child; (2) they must overcome internal inhibitors against acting on their motivation to abuse; (3) they must overcome external inhibitors against acting on their motivation to abuse; and (4) they must overcome children's resistance to their acting on their motivation to abuse. In many cases, perpetrators "overcome children's resistance" by engaging in behaviors that reduce the likelihood that children will demonstrate overt resistance to their abusive overtures. Thus, children need not overtly resist in order for a sexual relationship to be considered abusive, or in order for the abusive relationship to have traumatic consequences.

Finkelhor assumes that the four preconditions follow one another in a logical sequence, as indicated in Figure 1. For example, the overcoming of inhibitions to abusing children only becomes relevant if persons have previously developed a motivation to abuse children or a child.

Crucial for our analysis, Finkelhor also assumes that each of the four preconditions of child sexual abuse is comprised of both psychological and social factors (1984: 56). It may seem obvious that social factors can constitute external inhibitors that reduce the likelihood that persons who are motivated to abuse children and who have overcome internal inhibitions to acting on that motivation will successfully abuse children. For example, Finkelhor contends that lack of social supports for children's mothers can provide opportunities for motivated and disinhibited perpetrators to abuse children undetected and unsanctioned. However, Finkelhor maintains that social factors can also influence victims' ability to resist motivated and disinhibited perpetrators' advances. For example, he contends that children's immersion in cultural milieus that empower children to act on their own behalf increases their capacity to resist motivated and disinhibited perpetrators.

Perpetrator Develops Motivation to Abuse Children ⟶ Perpetrator Overcomes Internal Inhibitors against Abuse of Children ⟶ Perpetrator Overcomes External Inhibitors against Abuse of Children ⟶ Perpetrator Overcomes Victims' Resistance to Abuse

Figure 1 Finkelhor's four preconditions of child sexual abuse

Further, Finkelhor maintains that social factors also can influence motivated perpetrators' ability to overcome internal inhibitions against acting on their motivation to abuse children. For example, motivated perpetrators' immersion in cultural milieus in which sexual interest in children is tolerated increases their ability to overcome internal inhibitions. Finally, he maintains that social factors can even influence a person's motivation to abuse children. For example, persons immersed in cultural milieus in which masculinity is linked to being dominant and powerful in sexual relationships may be more likely to develop a motivation to abuse children. The belief that social factors can influence the likelihood that a person develops the motivation to abuse children and overcome inhibitions to acting on that motivation runs counter to theories that assume perpetrators are characterized by psychological defects of one kind or another (Ward and Siegert 2002), but is consistent with empirical evidence that persons who abuse children do not exhibit psychological profiles that are noticeably different from those who do not abuse children and evince low recidivism rates (Goldsworthy 2015; Hanson et al. 2018). Indeed, some believe that persons who develop the motivation to abuse children in particular social contexts, termed "situational abusers," far outnumber persons who possess an enduring overriding attraction to children, termed "preferential" abusers (Smallbone et al. 2008).

2.2 Applying Finkelhor's Four Preconditions Model to Organizational Contexts

We maintain that organizational structures are among the social factors that can influence each of Finkelhor's four preconditions of child sexual abuse that occurs in organizations. In the interests of streamlining our exposition, we will sometimes collapse the first two of Finkelhor's preconditions into a single precondition, referring to perpetrators as being "predisposed" to abuse children when they both possess the motivation to abuse children or a child and have overcome internal inhibitors against acting on that motivation. Our basic model is illustrated in Figure 2.

When applying Finkelhor's model to organizational contexts, a question arises as to whether or not perpetrators enter organizations with a preexisting motivation to abuse (Finkelhor's first precondition), with an awareness of that motivation, and having already overcome internal inhibitions against acting on that motivation (Finkelhor's second precondition). Prior research suggests that perpetrators of child sexual abuse in organizational contexts can be grouped into one of three categories in this regard (Lanning and Dietz 2014).

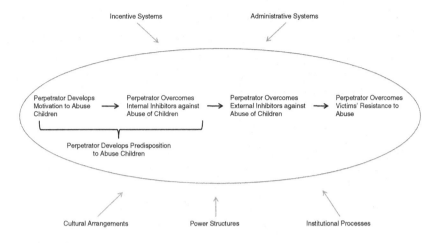

Figure 2 Model of the organizational determinants of child sexual abuse in organizational contexts

Some people enter these contexts possessing a motivation to abuse children, having an awareness of that motivation, and having already overcome internal inhibitions against acting on that motivation. Organizational structures can influence the opportunities that such people have to abuse children in organizations, where opportunity is a function of the likelihood that children will succumb to abusers' overtures (Finkelhor's fourth precondition) and the likelihood that abusers' overtures will go undetected and unpunished (Finkelhor's third precondition).

Other people enter these contexts already possessing a motivation to abuse children, but lacking an awareness of this motivation. These individuals discover their motivations to abuse children and find ways to overcome internal inhibitions against acting on the discovered motivations only after entering the organization. Organizational structures can influence the likelihood that such persons will discover their underlying motivation to abuse children, the likelihood that they will find ways to overcome internal inhibitions against doing so, and the likelihood that they will have the opportunity to abuse children in organizations.

Finally, still other people who abuse children enter organizations lacking a motivation to do so. These individuals develop the motivation to abuse children or a specific child and find ways to overcome inhibitions against acting on their motivation to abuse after entering the organization. Organizational structures influence the likelihood that such persons will develop a motivation to abuse children or a specific child, find ways to overcome internal inhibitions against abusing children, and have the opportunity to abuse children in organizations. The possibility that people discover or develop the motivation to abuse children or a specific child only *after* joining an organization is consistent with analyses of the etiology of other boundary violating sexual behaviors, such as therapist–client sexual relationships (Simon 1995).

2.3 Introducing Process Considerations into Finkelhor's Model

Finkelhor's four preconditions model does not consider the process through which child sexual abuse develops. Our reading of case studies and reporting on instances of child sexual abuse suggest that the process through which child sexual abuse takes shape can be characterized in the same way that other forms of misconduct develop in organizations (Palmer 2012). Specifically, we think that instances of child sexual abuse vary along two dimensions: the extent of prior social interaction that occurs between perpetrators and victims that lays a foundation for the abuse, and the degree to which perpetrators construct their behavior in a self-conscious and strategic fashion. Further, we think that the extreme positions along these two dimensions can be conceptualized as jointly constituting four Weberian "ideal typical" processes through which child sexual abuse can develop (Shils and Finch 2011).[4] Finally, we think that the extent to which an instance of child sexual abuse conforms to one or another of these four ideal types influences the ways in which organizational structures can facilitate abuse, inhibit detection of abuse, and undermine response to abuse.

Some perpetrators sexually abuse children without much prior social interaction laying the foundation for the abuse, and do so in a self-conscious and strategic fashion based on previously developed motivations and established means of overcoming internal inhibitions. The literature on child sexual abuse does not extensively analyze this ideal type of abuse, although it does report many instances of it. Physical force can facilitate this type of abuse. For example, adults or children can physically overpower their victims in the moment, as is the case when an adult or child rapes a child. But organizational structures also can facilitate this ideal type of abuse. For example, adults can obtain the compliance of their victims in the moment, as is the case when

---

[4] Weber envisioned "ideal types" as methodological constructs that facilitate the analysis of social phenomena, rather than as normative constructs indicating desirable social arrangements. Specifically, he conceptualized ideal types as having attributes that are characteristic of a social phenomenon, while allowing that not all of these attributes will manifest in every instance of the social phenomenon, and recognizing that some might manifest in other social phenomenon.

physicians such as Dr. Nassar represent their abusive behavior as consistent with medical profession norms (Bonesteel 2017).

Other perpetrators abuse children without much prior social interaction laying the foundation for the abuse, and in a less than fully self-conscious and strategic fashion. The literature on child sexual abuse does not extensively analyze this type of abuse either, although it does report numerous instances of it. We will show that organizational structures also can influence the likelihood that persons will perpetrate abuse in this way. For example, a student may succumb to informal group pressure and join in the abuse initiated by his/her peers against a fellow student.

Still other perpetrators abuse children after considerable prior social interaction laying the foundation for the abuse, and in a self-conscious and strategic fashion. The literature has devoted considerable attention to this type of abuse. Perpetrators who self-consciously and strategically orchestrate social interaction with victims with the intention to facilitate abuse are said to "groom" their victims. Grooming consists of a variety of tactics, such as performing favors, providing gifts, and sharing confidences with potential victims. Perpetrators groom potential victims to discern their capacity to resist sexual overtures and their inclination to expose such overtures to guardians in the environment. Perpetrators also groom potential victims to cultivate their emotional attachment and to acquire their guardians' trust. Finally, perpetrators groom potential victims to encourage them to understand the incipient abusive relationship as normative (Conte et al. 1989; Elliot et al. 1995). Organizational structures can facilitate this ideal type of abuse in many ways. For example, adults can orchestrate interaction with victims so as to cultivate the understanding that the abusive relationship is normative by portraying the incipient relationship as consistent with the organization's culture.

Finally, other perpetrators abuse children after considerable prior social interaction laying the foundation for the abuse, but in a less than fully self-conscious and strategic fashion. Such perpetrators can be said to drift into abusive relationships with children in a "crescive" fashion – that is, in a gradual, spontaneous, developmental manner. The literature on child sexual abuse has devoted relatively little attention to this ideal type of abuse. Perpetrators who drift into abusive relationships with children in a crescive fashion engage in the same behaviors as those who perpetrate abuse in a self-conscious and strategic fashion. Further, the behavior of persons who drift into abuse in a crescive fashion, like the behavior of those who perpetrate abuse in a self-conscious and strategic fashion, contributes to the construction of meaning, such that victims come to understand receptivity to the perpetrators' overtures as appropriate and even required. In addition, it is through enacting these behaviors that perpetrators incrementally discover or develop a motivation to abuse children or a specific child and find ways to overcome internal inhibitions to acting on their motivation.

We think three psychological mechanisms can facilitate the incremental disabling of internal inhibitions to acting on the crescive discovery or development of motivations to abuse children in organizations. First, people who perpetuate minor forms of misconduct for a period of time tend to become "desensitized" to the guilt they feel from doing so, freeing themselves to engage in more significant forms of misconduct (Ashforth and Anand 2003). Second, people who engage in minor forms of misconduct for a period of time also tend to develop post-hoc rationalizations of their wrongdoing, freeing themselves to engage in more significant forms of misconduct (Alicke and Sedikidis 2011; Staw 1976). Finally, people who engage in minor forms of misconduct tend to evaluate the ethicality of their behavior not in abstract terms, but rather relative to the ethicality of their prior behavior (Palmer 2012). Together, this suggests that people who engage in modest forms of misconduct place themselves on an emotional and cognitive slippery slope to more objectionable forms of misconduct in the future.

The process through which the motivation to abuse children is discovered and developed and internal inhibitions against abusing children are overcome is likely to depart from what one might otherwise consider a logical progression. Thus, in cases where younger adults develop sexual relationships with children, such as when a young teacher abuses an older middle school or high school student, perpetrators have been characterized as exhibiting "bad judgment" or a "misplaced sense of privilege" (Shakeshaft 2004, 2014). Similarly, in cases where children develop sexual relationships with younger peers, such as when a boy in his junior year of high school and over the legal age of consent develops a sexual relationship with a girl who is a freshman and below the age of consent (a so-called Romeo and Juliet relationship), perpetrators may be partially ignorant of social norms and the law (Stillman 2016).

Organizational structures also can facilitate this fourth ideal type of abuse in many ways. For example, day care facility job descriptions may encourage staff to interact with children in a physically intimate manner, which can increase the likelihood that staff will discover or develop the motivation to abuse children or a specific child. We suspect that the fundamental tendency to view all human behavior, including unethical behavior, as rational (Bazerman and Tenbrunsel 2011) leads social workers, law enforcement officials, and scholars of various stripes to overestimate the frequency with which perpetrators consciously groom their victims and thus underestimate the frequency with which child sexual abuse unfolds in a crescive fashion.

Now that we have delineated a framework according to which organizational structures can influence the four preconditions of child sexual abuse in organizational contexts, we proceed with an in-depth analysis of the role that five specific organizational structures can play in child sexual abuse in organizations.

3 Incentive and Administrative Systems

3.1 Incentive Systems

Organizational theorists have devoted considerable attention to analyzing the impact that incentive systems have on organizational participant behavior and have developed models of employee motivation, of which "expectancy theory" is the dominant model (Nadler and Lawler 1977). It holds that employees are motivated to pursue behaviors to the extent that they (1) value the rewards or eschew the punishments that can follow from enacting the behaviors, referred to as "outcome valence," (2) expect that they are capable of enacting those behaviors, referred to as "effort-performance expectancy," and (3) expect that they will be rewarded or escape punishment for doing so, referred to as "performance-outcome expectancy."[5]

The literature on child sexual abuse in organizational contexts devotes considerable attention to the role that incentives play in the perpetration, detection, and response to child sexual abuse, albeit concentrating primarily on adult–child abuse. Much attention focuses on the "outcome valence" component of expectancy theory – specifically, the underlying psychological conditions that lead people to value sexual relationships with children (Finkelhor's first precondition). For example, Ward and Siegert (2002) offer an influential analysis that identifies five "pathways" to child sexual abuse: intimacy and social skills deficits, distorted sexual scripts, emotional dysregulation, cognitive distortions, and a unique combination of these four pathways that corresponds with pedophilia.

Some consideration is given to the "effort-performance expectancy" component of expectancy theory – specifically, the factors that influence the likelihood that persons predisposed to abuse children believe that they can overcome children's resistance to their advances (Finkelhor's fourth precondition). For example, it is believed that all children are vulnerable to abuse due to

---

[5] The organizational participants in youth-serving organizations can be employees or volunteers. We do not distinguish between these two kinds of organizational participants in this Element and use the terms "organizational participant," "member," and "people" interchangeably throughout, although we acknowledge that incentives (and other organizational structures) may influence employees and volunteers in different ways.

their physical and cognitive development (Irenyi et al. 2006). But it is thought that some children are particularly vulnerable, including children with physical and cognitive disabilities, low self-esteem, weak familial and social attachments, and prior victimization (Conte et al. 1989; Elliot et al. 1995; Wurtle 2012).

Finally, concern is also given to the "performance-outcome expectancy" component of expectancy theory – specifically, the factors that influence the likelihood that persons predisposed to abuse children believe that they can do so undetected and unpunished (Finkelhor's third precondition). For example, it is believed that perpetrators enjoy freedom from detection in situations in which there are few third-party observers or when there are few third parties to whom victims can report their abuse (Smallbone et al. 2008).

There is ample evidence that persons predisposed to abuse children seek to join organizations where opportunities are prevalent and, once they have gained entry to an organization, attempt to redesign the organization to maximize these opportunities (Colton et al. 2010; Wurtele 2012). For example, a convicted sex offender recently "posed as an employee" of the Washington, D.C., public school district and drove a bus that transported students with disabilities to and from school, presumably to gain access to the vulnerable students (Balingit 2017). Further, there is evidence that employees who are predisposed to abuse children are more likely to do so when they believe the risk of detection is minimal (Auriol and Brilon 2014).

Some factors that influence potential perpetrators' opportunity to abuse children are tangential to the other organizational structures considered in this monograph. For example, an organization's physical design influences employees' opportunity to abuse (e.g., in the case of a childcare facility, whether it is subdivided into multiple rooms with doors, which afford potential abusers the opportunity to abuse children undetected). Other factors that influence potential perpetrators' opportunity to abuse children, though, are related to the other organizational structures considered here. We discuss how power structures, administrative systems, cultural arrangements, and institutional processes can influence employees' opportunities to sexually abuse children, as well as how these structures and processes can influence the other determinants of abuse, in the following sections of the monograph. Before moving on to this task, though, we note two other implications that expectancy theory holds for child sexual abuse in organizations.

First, expectancy theory suggests an additional mechanism through which the opportunity to abuse children may influence the likelihood of abuse in organizational contexts. Finkelhor's (1984) four preconditions model, like almost all scholarship on child sexual abuse, assumes that motivation and opportunity are separate factors regulating the likelihood of abuse. Specifically, Finkelhor's model assumes that some people possess the predisposition to abuse children and that the situations in which such persons find themselves, most importantly, the strength of external inhibitors and the effectiveness of victims' resistance, determine whether or not they act on their predisposition. Expectancy theory, though, assumes that motivation is a function of opportunity – that is, it assumes that people become motivated to engage in a behavior to the extent they expect that they can enact the behavior and will receive a reward or escape punishment if they do so. This implies that Finkelhor's four preconditions of child sexual abuse may not be just linked in a linear logical progression but also may be causally related to one another such that weak external inhibitors of abuse and ineffective victim resistance increase the likelihood that people develop and act on the predisposition to abuse children. These causal relationships are depicted in Figure 3.

More specifically, expectancy theory suggests that people may enter organizations and crescively develop a disposition to sexually abuse children at least partly because they have an increasing opportunity to do so. For example, teachers may develop the motivation to pursue sexual relationships with students partly because their environment is predominantly filled with students, some of these students develop personal attachments to them, and their opportunities to interact with these students unsupervised grow apace of the students' personal attachment. Thus, there are instances of teacher–student abuse in which the student appears to have initiated a personal relationship with a teacher, albeit possibly unaware of the potential for the personal relationship to develop into a sexual one (Mettler 2016).

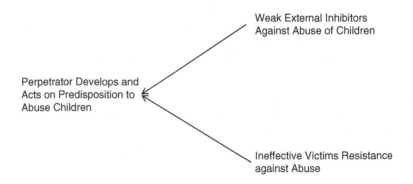

Figure 3 Finkelhor's preconditions of child sexual abuse: causally reconfigured

Second, expectancy theory may partially account for four well-established statistics in the domain of sexual assault generally, which likely have analogs in the narrower domain of child sexual abuse in organizations. In doing so, it suggests a feedback loop between the detection and response to child sexual abuse on the one hand, and the perpetration of abuse on the other. The vast majority (by some estimates 80–90 percent) of all instances of sexual assault go unreported (Lonsway and Archambault 2012). Further, the vast majority (by some estimates, 82–86 percent) of all reported instances of sexual assault go unprosecuted (Bouffard 2000; Patterson and Campbell 2010; Spohn, Beichner, and Davids-Frenzel 2001). What is more, the vast majority (by one estimate 82 percent) of all prosecutions for rape (the most serious form of sexual assault) do not result in convictions. Finally, a significant percentage of women (by one estimate 18 percent) have been raped in their lifetime (Kilpatrick et al. 2007).

It is possible that the low incidence of reporting, prosecution, and conviction of sexual assault is interrelated, and that these patterns may inform the behaviors of sexual assault perpetrators. It is well accepted that victims of sexual assault eschew reporting their assaults partly because they have low expectations that the reports will be acted upon, and successfully prosecuted if acted upon (Lisak et al. 2010). Further, it is believed that prosecutors pursue only a minority of reported instances of sexual assault because they have low expectations that their efforts will result in conviction (Krakauer 2015). Finally, it is widely recognized that men at least develop and act on the predisposition to sexually assault women partly because they have low expectations of being punished (Schewe and O'Donohue 1996). If these relationships hold for child sexual abuse in organizations, it suggests that the perpetration, detection, and response to abuse are tightly coupled. More specifically, it suggests that any organizational structure that influences the detection or response to abuse, including those discussed in subsequent sections of this Element, will have a significant indirect effect on the perpetration of abuse.

3.2 Administrative Systems

Administrative systems also coordinate behavior in formal organizations. Administrative systems establish a division of labor, in which tasks are subdivided and assigned to separate subunits. They also delineate preferred practices and routines such as rules and standard operating procedures that specify how organizational participants should complete the subdivided tasks. Finally, administrative systems elaborate procedures for monitoring and enforcing organizational participant compliance with preferred practices and routines (March and Simon 1958).

The literature on child sexual abuse in organizations devotes considerable attention to the role that administrative systems play in abuse. Many contend that inadequate job applicant-screening procedures, which fail to include probing interviews, the solicitation of references from prior employers, or even criminal record checks, can allow persons predisposed to sexually abuse children to enter an organization, thus increasing children's risk of abuse (cf. Cashmore et al. 2016). For example, Jacqui Barnat, the children's services manager for the southern region of YMCA NSW in Australia, hired Jonathan Lord to work at the Caringbah Out of School Hours Care (OSHC) facility without subjecting him to a thorough background check. In fact, she did not even seek a reference from another YMCA organization that employed Lord as a camp counselor in the United States. As a result, she failed to unearth the fact that Lord had been dismissed from his camp counselor post because of suspected abuse of a young camper. Within two years of his employment at the Caringbah OSHC facility, Lord had sexually abused several children (Royal Commission Case Study No. 2).

Others maintain that lax or ill-conceived employee and volunteer behavior guidelines can provide persons predisposed to abuse children with opportunities to act on their predispositions. For example, childcare centers in which it is standard operating procedure for workers to change children's diapers one-on-one in closed rooms provide workers with the opportunity to abuse children undetected. Lax or ill-conceived behavior guidelines can also fail to prohibit behavior that may constitute abuse or grooming (Erooga, Allnock, and Telford 2012). Obviously, guidelines that fail to prohibit abuse or grooming implicitly authorize perpetrators to abuse or groom children. Less obviously, guidelines that fail to prohibit behavior that may constitute abuse or grooming can impede the detection of abuse, because they make it difficult for third parties who observe permitted but problematic behaviors to know whether they are observing abuse or grooming. This may have been the case at the Caringbah OSHC facility in New South Wales, Australia, where Jonathan Lord abused twelve children. The Caringbah OSHC's *Staff Handbook* for its Holiday Adventures Program advised childcare workers:

> You are doing a good job when . . . your children are always hanging on you, holding your hand, or asking for piggyback rides.   (Case Study No. 2, 28)

One of Lord's coworkers, Alicia Dellaca, testified that she saw him engaging in behavior that many would consider indicative of grooming, but did not report his behavior to her superior because she did not perceive it to be inappropriate in the OSHC context. In her testimony to the Royal Commission, she stated:

> On reflection, John did sometimes have children on his lap. At the time I didn't think it was suspicious by itself, but I did think that it wasn't a good look, as it made it look to the other children that he had favourites.
>
> (Case Study No. 2, 62)

Further, we suspect that guidelines that fail to prohibit behavior that may constitute abuse or grooming also can permit organizational participants to engage in behaviors that increase the likelihood that persons unaware of their predisposition to abuse children will discover their predisposition; and those who do not possess a predisposition to abuse children will develop a predisposition to abuse. For example, it appears to have been standard operating procedure in some Queensland, Australia, swim clubs in the 1980s for coaches to give athletes massages in closed rooms (Case Study No. 15). It seems possible that coaches who followed such procedures could discover their predisposition to abuse children or develop a predisposition to do so in the course of enacting those procedures.

The literature on child sexual abuse in organizations also focuses attention on inadequate policies and procedures related to the detection of and response to child sexual abuse. For example, the subdivision of tasks that allocates responsibility for monitoring organizational participant behavior to specialized roles may limit the number of eyes available to uncover instances of abuse. Additionally, ineffective communication channels can impede interpretation of isolated bits of information that emerge in different parts of the organization that, if integrated, might constitute signs of abuse. Finally, absence of explicit rules and expectations regarding what constitutes child sexual abuse can undermine the response of those who become aware of abuse allegations. In the assessment of Professor Stephen Smallbone, these and a number of cultural factors to be discussed in the next section impeded the detection of Jonathan Lord's abuse of children at the Caringbah OHSC (Case Study No. 2: 70).

Having briefly discussed two organizational structures to which the literature on child sexual abuse has devoted reasonably thorough attention, we turn in the next three sections to a discussion of organizational structures that the literature has yet to consider in a comprehensive fashion: power structures, cultural arrangements, and institutional processes.

4 Power Structures

Formal organizations also coordinate and control organizational participant behavior through power structures. The literature on child sexual abuse recognizes that power plays a role in child sexual abuse. Indeed, the World Health Organization (2006) considers a power differential between perpetrators and victims to be a defining condition of child sexual abuse. But, the analysis of the role that power plays in abuse remains underdeveloped. We define power as the capacity to get what one wants over the resistance of others (Weber 1946).[6] And we distinguish between two kinds of power in organizations: formal authority, rooted in the hierarchical chain of command, and informal power, rooted in the control of resources (Mechanic 1962).

4.1 Formal Authority

Formal authority is derived from one's position in the chain of command. The higher people are in the chain of command, the more formal authority they possess. Positions in the chain of command provide their occupants with formal power to the extent that the system of authority and position-occupants are considered legitimate. Systems of authority can derive legitimacy from three logics: charismatic, traditional, and rational/legal logics (i.e., competency or ownership). Position-occupants can derive legitimacy from being successful at assigned tasks and by manipulating subordinates' rewards and punishments. When systems of authority and position-occupants are considered legitimate, the norm of obedience to authority is strong. And when the norm of obedience to authority is strong, it can override other imperatives, such as rational calculations and normative assessments. This is well illustrated by Stanley Milgram's (1974) laboratory experiments, in which subjects tended to obey the instructions of people they believed were scientific authorities, even when the instructions required them to administer what they believed were painful and even dangerous electrical shocks to fellow subjects.

The literature on child sexual abuse in organizations devotes considerable attention to the role that formal authority plays in child sexual abuse. Many recognize that formal power can facilitate abuse. For example, Cense and Brackenridge (2001) observed that coaches in the sporting organizations they studied possessed formal power over the young athletes in their charge which made it difficult for the athletes "to challenge or resist the [abusive] behavior of their seniors" (68). Formal authority may have enabled Stephen Roser to abuse swimmers in his charge at the Scone Swimming Club in New South Wales, Australia. Roser was the swimming club's head coach and the club's athletes likely felt obliged to follow his orders. Thus, when Rosen instructed survivor AEB to float stomach down in the water in front of him and to wrap her thighs around his hips and stroke with her arms without using her legs, she complied.

---

[6] Power has been characterized in many other ways (cf., Foucault 1976). We do not explore these other characterizations of power here, because they are less frequently employed in the organizations literature. But we acknowledge that they may be useful in extending the arguments presented here.

And when he proceeded to touch AEB under her bathing suit, she apparently did not overtly resist (Case Study No. 15). Further, coaches in sporting organizations can punish child athletes who resist their abusive advances. A chorus of former UK youth soccer players recently claimed that they were abused as children by their former youth team coaches. And some recounted that when they resisted the abuse, the coaches held them out of matches (Bennhold 2016).

Many also recognize that formal power can suppress victim reports of abuse. For example, Cense and Brackenridge (2001) observed that athletes who are victims of child sexual abuse do not report the abuse they experience at the hands of their coaches partly because they fear "losing their place in the sport" (70). Formal authority may have suppressed the reporting of child sexual abuse at the Geelong Grammar School, an independent Anglican boarding and day school in Victoria, Australia. Abuse survivor BKV testified that he did not report the abuse he experienced at the hands of a Geelong teacher because "he did not feel that he would be safe if he reported the abuse" (Case Study No. 32, 10). And when survivor BKO did report abuse he experienced at the school, he "found the subsequent process very threatening" (Case Study No. 32: 10). Indeed, formal authority may even be used to prohibit reporting. One student at the Geelong School was admonished to remain silent and was expelled from the school after he discussed the abuse with a peer (Case Study No. 32: 14).

Finally, third-party observers may decline reporting abuse perpetrated by superiors because they fear retribution. Formal authority and associated fears of retribution appear to have suppressed third-party reporting of an instance of child sexual abuse at Pennsylvania State University (PSU), where former assistant football coach Jerry Sandusky abused a child in a university shower room. A witnessing janitor, despite being severely shaken, declined to report the abuse to his superiors. He knew that Sandusky was a former associate of head football coach Joe Paterno, understood that Paterno occupied a position of considerable formal power at PSU, and feared that filing a report against Sandusky would provoke Paterno's ire. As he testified, reporting the incident "would have been like going against the President of the United States . . . I know Paterno has so much power, if he wanted to get rid of someone, I would have been gone" (Jones 2012).

Third-party observers may be reluctant to report child sexual abuse perpetrated by superiors or peers, even if they believe that those above them in the hierarchy to whom they might report the abuse will be inclined to simply ignore their reports. Hence, one of Jonathan Lord's coworkers at the Caringbah OSHC facility who was suspicious of his behavior testified that she did not feel comfortable raising concerns about a coworker with her manager because she "didn't trust her and I was worried that if I raised an issue with her, she wouldn't take it further" (Case Study No. 2, 71). When third-party observers raise concerns about a superior or peer and these concerns are not taken seriously, the reporting individual risks retaliation by the abuser's peers and protectors.

Some recognize that the characteristics of authority systems can play a role in child sexual abuse, although their analyses of these characteristics are not as deep as they could be. For example, some warn that organizations run by "charismatic" leaders are exposed to a heightened risk of child sexual abuse (Coates 1997; Timmerman and Schreuder 2014). They do not, though, explain why charismatic authority is more problematic than other types of authority. We think charismatic authority is problematic because it, like traditional authority, provides those who possess it with wider leeway in the command of subordinates. Rational/legal principles, which legitimate systems of authority in the private sector, offer formal authorities relatively little leeway in the command of subordinates. Managers of for-profit firms can only legitimately order their subordinates to engage in work-related actions (e.g., they can order subordinates to answer a customer complaint, but not to wash their personal car). Charismatic and traditional logics, which legitimate systems of authority in religious and some other types of organizations, offer formal authorities relatively more leeway in the command of subordinates. Priests, rabbis, and clerics can instruct their followers how to think and act in domains such as work, family, and interpersonal relationships that are well beyond the place of worship. The charismatic and traditional authority enjoyed by Catholic priests likely underpinned their ability to perpetrate the abuse that came to light at the turn of the twenty-first century (Boston Globe 2002).

Further, some warn of the dangers of "hierarchical organizations" (Sprober et al. 2014; Staller 2012). They do not, though, elaborate what the hierarchical configuration is or why it, as opposed to other configurations, is problematic. We suspect that a number of dimensions along which systems of formal authority vary and that some implicitly equate with hierarchy can play a role in child sexual abuse. Specifically, we suspect that organizations with unitary chains of command – that is, in which subordinates have a single superior – are more susceptible to the perpetration of child sexual abuse, especially when they do not have a separate subunit adequately empowered to address subordinate complaints. For example, Jimmy Sevile, who sexually abused more than seventy women, girls, and boys over the course of his forty-year career at the British Broadcasting Corporation (BBC), is believed to have escaped accountability for his behavior partly due to the BBC's "hierarchical structure, the impracticability of complaining to anyone other than a line manager, and the weakness of the personnel department" (De Freytas-Tamura 2016).

Other dimensions along which systems of formal authority can vary may also play a role in child sexual abuse in organizations – in particular, the narrowness of the span of control, the strength of the norm of obedience to authority, and the degree to which officeholders are viewed as legitimate by virtue of their reputation for competence and/or the control of rewards and punishments. We discuss these three factors in more detail in Section 7 in connection with total institutions.

4.2   Informal Power

Informal power is derived from the control of resources. The more resources people control, the more informal power they possess. The control of resources provides people with informal power to the extent that their control over resources is decisive and the resources are scarce and important. Resources can encompass a wide range of things that can be grouped under the umbrella of French and Raven's (1959) categorization of power bases (e.g., information, expertise). When people possess decisive control over scarce important resources, others in the organization who are dependent upon them for access to those resources will yield to their expressed and inferred wishes.

The literature on child sexual abuse in organizational contexts for the most part ignores the role that informal power plays in child sexual abuse, even though its effects on the perpetration, detection, and response to abuse in organizations are likely as pervasive as the effects of formal power. For example, we think that informal power can facilitate the abuse of children, especially peer abuse insofar as peer power differentials are almost always exclusively the result of differential resource control. Informal power differentials between children are often rooted in the relative ages of children, which are correlated with the relative possession of physical strength and allies. Informal power may have played a role in a swimmer's sexual abuse by an older athlete at the Clovelly Surf Lifesaving Club in New South Wales, Australia. Survivor AEA testified that he was repeatedly abused against his will by the older, presumably stronger, and apparently more popular teammate Terrance Buck (Case Study No. 15).

We also think that informal power can impede the detection of abuse in organizations. Informal power can deter victims from reporting abuse. This appears to have been the case with Andrew Woodward, a professional soccer player who eschewed reporting the abuse he experienced as a child at the hands of his youth coach. The young Woodward depended on the coach for positive evaluations to facilitate his progression in the sport and the coach won Woodward's silence by reminding him that he "could ruin (his) football tomorrow" and by warning him to "keep quiet or you're finished" (Bennhold 2016). Informal power may also deter third parties from reporting abuse. Staff who discover superiors or peers engaged in abuse may be reluctant to come forward if they believe that the perpetrators possess power in the form of scarce and important expertise. This may be another reason why coworkers of Jonathan Lord failed to report their suspicions that Lord was abusing children at the Caringbah OSHC facility. Although hired as a part-time casual worker, over a period of time Lord advanced to the position of full-time coordinator. As such, he had longer tenure and more experience in the facility than his assistants, likely giving him more informal power than they possessed. Thus, childcare assistant Michelle Bates is reported to have testified that

> she once felt uncomfortable, as she observed physical interaction between Lord and a child which she considered involved unnecessary touching. She knew that unnecessary touching was wrong but she did not tell anyone about the incident. She assumed that Lord "was a more senior person because of his attitude" and she "just didn't feel like I was in a place to say anything". (Case Study No. 2, 63)

Finally, we think informal power can reduce the likelihood that reports of sexual abuse will produce effective organizational responses. If those suspected of perpetrating child sexual abuse possess informal power, others in the organization will be reluctant to take up and pursue the case against them. Informal power likely plays a role in the suppression of reports received by managers of sporting clubs and parents of their athletes. Several researchers note that the managers of sporting clubs and even the parents of their athletes may be reluctant to pursue investigations and criminal charges against coaches alleged to have perpetrated sexual abuse when the coaches are successful, because successful coaches possess unique skills and scarce recruiting contacts at the next competitive level that managers and parents consider important and scarce (Brackenridge and Kirby 1997; Parent and Bannon 2012). Hence, survivors who testified to having been sexually abused by Scott Volkers while he was a coach at several Queensland, Australia, swimming clubs indicated that they did not report the abuse to senior club officials, because they doubted that the officials would act on their allegations as Volkers was considered a particularly talented coach. This belief appears to have been borne out by subsequent events, insofar as Volkers was allowed to remain active at the highest levels of the coaching ranks for many years despite having been the subject of repeated allegations of abuse (Case Study No. 15).

4.2.1   Power Rituals

Power, whether it is based on one's position in the chain of command or one's control of resources, is most efficiently utilized when it is recognized and submitted to, without first being translated into influence. Translating power into influence consumes time and energy. It also engenders opposition that must be addressed, which consumes additional time and energy (Pfeffer 1981). But to be recognized, power on occasion must be displayed. Powerful people sometimes display their power by conducting rituals, which entail placing subordinates or dependent persons in situations where they are constrained to act out the role of the powerless (Moch and Huff 1983).

It is well established that sexual harassment and sexual assault are often not about "sex," but rather about "power." That is, those who engage in sexual harassment and even rape, either consciously or intuitively, understand that these behaviors have the effect of valorizing their power and increasing voluntary compliance in the future (Filipovic 2013; Goleman 1991). Child sexual abuse can serve the same purpose. In the case of peer abuse, it can be a means by which peer group leaders in youth-serving organizations reinforce their informal power over their peers. For example, groups of older children sexually abused isolated younger peers at Geelong Grammar School (Case Study No. 32). And the abuse perpetrated by the older students (in one case, penetrating a student's anal canal with a hockey stick) appears to have been motivated by the desire to dominate the younger peers rather than a desire to gratify sexual impulses (McKenzie-Murray 2015). In the case of adult–child sexual abuse, abuse can be a means by which staff members in a youth-serving organization display and thus reaffirm their formal authority over their charges. This appears to have been the case in the boarding schools established to assimilate Native American youth into mainstream US society at the turn of the nineteenth century (Smith 2004).

4.2.2   Power as a Cause of Child Sexual Abuse

There is a substantial and growing body of theory and research that reveals how the possession of power, whether based on position in the chain of command or control of resources, leads people to treat others over whom they possess power unethically. Kipnis (1972) was the first to empirically demonstrate that the possession and wielding of power can lead people to treat others unethically. Lee-Chai, Chen, and Chartrand (2001) describe recent research that shows the possession and wielding of power can increase a powerful person's propensity to engage in a wide range of unethical behaviors, including sexually aggressive behaviors. Power appears to cause those who possess it to view themselves as morally superior (and thus worthy of ethical license) and to view others over whom they possess power as morally inferior (and thus unworthy of ethical treatment). Power also appears to cause those who possess it to view those over whom they possess power as less distinct and, importantly, with less distinct rights. Finally, power also appears to cause those who possess it to become desensitized to social disapproval – in particular, social disapproval for treating others unethically (Keltner, Gruenfeld, and Anderson 2003). We think that the amount of power a person possesses over children may be positively related to the motivation the person has to sexually abuse the children over whom they have power. It is hard, though, to disentangle power as cause of abusive motivation from power as facilitator of abusive motivation in actual instances of child sexual abuse. Thus, we refrain from offering illustrations of this postulated tendency.

4.2.3   Interorganizational Power Relations and Elite Networks

Organizations typically are situated in environments composed of other organizations upon which they are dependent for the supply of resources, both tangible and intangible, and these dependencies constitute interorganizational power relations (Pfeffer and Salancik 1978). Organizations depend on a range of suppliers who provide capital, labor, and material (both inanimate and human) to be processed. They also depend on customers, who purchase their products and services. Finally, they depend on a range of organizations that provide them with legitimacy, such as industry certifying bodies and government agencies. In addition, organizational leaders often maintain social relationships with the leaders of other organizations in their environment and, in doing so, build elite social networks. Elite social networks may have their roots in interorganizational power relationships, as is the case when the leader of one organization establishes a social relationship with the leader of another on which it is dependent, so as to manage that dependency. But elite social networks may have an independent rationale, providing a means for organizational elites to advance their own interests as individuals and as a class (Mintz and Schwartz 1985; Perruci and Pilisuk 1970).

We believe interorganizational power relations and elite social networks can influence the response to child sexual abuse in organizations. Specifically, we think that youth-serving organizations can use their power over other organizations in their environments and that leaders of youth-serving organizations can use their connections to the leaders of other organizations to protect themselves from external scrutiny and enforcement. For example, the Catholic Church in Boston possessed substantial organizational power by virtue of its authority over local educational institutions, its control of local nonprofit service organizations, its influence over philanthropic donations to these and other social service organizations, and its sway over parishioners' political allegiances. Further, Church leaders mingled with Boston's political, economic, and social elite, many of whom were members of the Catholic Church, products of its local parishes and educational institutions, and deeply involved in the Church and its affiliated organizations such as the Catholic Schools Foundation and Catholic Charities.

The Church is believed to have used its interorganizational power and the social connections of its leaders to successfully lobby elected officials to block legislation that threatened to eliminate its immunity to civil and criminal prosecution. As a result, the Catholic Church was able to preserve its autonomy in the investigation and adjudication of child sexual abuse allegations, and autonomy in its punishment and rehabilitation of confirmed abusers (Formicola 2016). Further, it is believed to have used its interorganizational power and its leader's social ties to suppress evidence that Church priests were sexually abusing children in local parishes. When instances of child sexual abuse perpetrated by priests were reported to Boston law enforcement authorities, police officers, prosecutors, and judges failed to follow up on these reports (Boston Globe 2002). When information about instances of abuse perpetrated by priests found its way to local media, print journalists failed to write articles and broadcast journalists failed to file stories about them (Knopf 2016). It was not until a religious and geographic outsider was hired as editor of the *Boston Globe* (Marty Baron, a Jewish newspaper executive who had grown up in Florida and had previously worked at the *New York Times* and the *Los Angeles Times*) that *The Globe* pursued the case of a Catholic priest who had abused over hundred children and, in doing so, ignited the Catholic Church sex abuse scandal in the United States.

4.2.4 A Tangent on Status

Sociologists define status as the relative rank that individuals occupy in a group. Because status and power often go hand in hand, the literature on child sexual abuse in organizations typically equates the two. But a person's rank in a group can derive from a multitude of factors other than power, including demonstrated skill at valued tasks, achievement of prized goals, membership in groups believed to possess superior attributes, and celebrity more generally. People who enjoy high status tend to receive deference from others, although they also sometimes shoulder increased duties and responsibilities (Weber 1946). Perhaps most important from the standpoint of child sexual abuse, high-status persons are more likely to obtain compliance to behavioral requests as well as receive the benefit of the doubt when making truth claims. The more status a person possesses vis-à-vis another person, the greater is their ability to sexually abuse the other person. Further, the more status a person possesses vis-à-vis another person, the greater is their ability to fend off the other person's accusations of guilt. In most developed societies, adults possess higher status than children and men possess higher status than women, factors that we discuss later in connection with organizational culture. But people may vary with respect to status by virtue of many other non-age and non-gender-related factors that can augment a person's capacity to abuse children and rebuff their allegations of abuse.

Adults may vary in their status by virtue of their role in an organization or their membership in professions. Elevated positions in the organizational chain of command convey status. Being a member of a profession (e.g., the medical profession), especially an elite segment of a profession (e.g., being a medical doctor rather than a physical therapist), also conveys status. And both sources of status provide organizational participants with increased opportunities to abuse others and rebuff accusations of abuse. In addition, achieving success in one's organizational role or professional position affords organizational participants similar benefits, should they be predisposed to abuse children. Dr. Larry Nassar's status as an elite sports medicine physician may have enabled him to abuse more than hundred youth athletes, as well as rebuff numerous allegations of abuse over a period of twenty years (Hobson 2017). Children may vary in status by virtue of their age and their achievement in the area of sports or other endeavors valued by their peers. And elevated status may provide children with increased opportunities to abuse their peers and rebuff accusations of abuse.

The interrelationship between status and power and their joint role in child sexual abuse in organizations are well illustrated by the case of BBC personality Jimmy Savile. His fame as a television host for youth-oriented programs and as a supporter of philanthropic causes, which earned him knighthood by both Queen Elizabeth II and Pope John Paul II, afforded Savile status that likely facilitated his abuse of children at the BBC and other organizations with which he was affiliated (such as orphanages for "troubled youth"). It also likely allowed him to rebuff the allegations of his lower-status victims. Further, his power as a source of revenue for the

BBC and as a point of entry into the broadcasting profession for aspiring talent allowed him to groom, overcome, and ensure the silence of his victims. These attributes also likely allowed him to deter coworkers and even superiors from reporting his activities, which were an "open secret" at the BBC (Bilefsky 2016; Burns and Cowell 2013; De Freytas-Tamura 2016).

5 Cultural Arrangements

5.1 Culture

Formal organizations also coordinate member behavior through cultural arrangements. The literature devotes considerable attention to the role that cultural arrangements play in the perpetration, detection, and response to abuse in organizations. But it typically misunderstands the nature and impact of culture. In some instances, culture is conceptualized as the pattern of behavior analysts seek to explain, as is the case when organizations where children have been abused are said to possess a culture of abuse. In other instances, organizational culture is defined expansively to include other organizational structures that can influence child sexual abuse, such as incentive systems, power structures, or administrative systems (discussed earlier) and institutional processes (discussed later). Thus, we preface our analysis of the role of culture with a brief review of theories of culture and the development of a framework for cultural analysis.[7]

5.2 An Integrated Conceptualization of Organizational Culture

Giorgi, Lockwood, and Glynn (2015) present a comprehensive review of theories of culture found in organizational theory. They distinguish between five principal conceptualizations of culture: values, stories, frames, toolkits, and categories. Values are what people "prefer, hold dear, or desire." Stories are "verbal or written narratives with causally linked sequences of events" that convey meaning. Frames are "filters or brackets that delimit what we pay attention to." Toolkits are "sets of stories, frames, categories, rituals, and practices that actors draw upon to make meaning or take action." Categories are "social constructions or classifications that define and structure the conceptual distinctions between objects, people, and practices" (Giorgi, Lockwood, and Glynn 2015: 5–7).

All five conceptualizations of culture identified by Giorgi, Lockwood, and Glynn are useful in understanding the role of organizational culture in child

---

[7] Much of this section is excerpted from Palmer and Feldman (2017).

sexual abuse in organizational contexts. Further, we think all five can be integrated into an overarching framework. In this framework, organizational culture is understood to possess both content and form. Cultural content consists of assumptions, values and beliefs, and norms that distinguish appropriate from inappropriate attitudes and behaviors. Assumptions are shared understandings about the categories that objects, people, and practices in the organization occupy (e.g., in a boarding school, whether students are considered trustworthy or untrustworthy) and the frame (or logic) according to which action in the organization unfolds (e.g., in a boarding school, whether the school is considered an educational endeavor or a business enterprise, and thus whether teachers' relationship to students is that of mentor or service provider). Values and beliefs are shared understandings about what constitutes virtuous or unscrupulous attitudes or behaviors in the organization (for example, whether or not it is good for teachers to interact with students as equals). Norms are shared understandings about what one should or should not think and do in the organization (for example, whether or not teachers should closely monitor coworkers' behavior).

Cultural forms consist of artifacts and practices that convey cultural content in an organization. Artifacts are the identifiable units in which cultural content can be conveyed. They can be material, such as the desks, chairs, accessories, and their arrangement in an organization's offices. For example, organizations that employ "open office" designs convey the assumption that social interaction in the organization is egalitarian. They also can be immaterial, such as the jargon, stories, and songs that an organization's members use and share. For example, organizations that employ jargon that refers to customers in a demeaning way convey the assumption that they are worthy of exploitation. Of course, immaterial artifacts such as jargon may sometimes leave material traces, such as when jargon is used in email correspondence. Practices are recurrent patterns of social interaction that convey cultural content, sometimes through the incorporation of artifacts. For example, after-work socials, during which organization-specific jargon may be used, may convey the norm that coworkers should develop friendships with one another.

This framework allows that cultural content and the forms that convey it can emerge spontaneously in the course of organizational participants' efforts to carry out their assigned responsibilities. But it also allows that cultural content and forms can be marshaled and even manufactured by powerful organizational actors to support their strategic objectives.

5.3   The Role of Organizational Culture in Child Sexual Abuse

5.3.1   Cultural Understandings of Gender Differences

The cultures of youth-serving organizations often contain content pertaining to their members' gender identities. In contemporary societies, youth-serving organizations tend to contain "patriarchal" content that includes the assumption that men are inherently active while women are passive; the value that men's activeness and women's passivity is good; and the norm that men and women should enact these differing levels of self-actualization. These cultural elements allow men greater opportunity to act and assign greater significance to their actions (Butler 1993). Hence, research shows that in mixed-gender groups, women are afforded fewer opportunities to speak and women's words are given less credence (Hancock and Rubin 2014; Zimmerman and West 1996). When the cultures of youth-serving organizations incorporate these cultural elements, they undermine effective response to child sexual abuse. Instances of abuse are typically detected by lower-level workers, who must make credible reports about the abuse to persons above them in the organization's hierarchy in order to trigger effective response. However, in most contemporary societies, men tend to fill upper-level positions in organizations, while women tend to occupy lower-level positions (Weinger 2015; Wilson 2009). As a result, many detected instances of child sexual abuse fail to trigger robust institutional responses simply because they are observed by women and communicated to men (Green 2001; Parkin and Green 1997).

Further, the cultures of some youth-serving organizations also contain "macho" content, which represents an extension of patriarchal content. Macho cultures feature the assumption that men and boys are innately aggressive, powerful, and competent, rather than submissive, helpless, and victimized, and include the norm that men should eschew self-concepts that acknowledge weakness, helplessness, and victimization. Macho cultures also embrace the assumption that boys are naturally aggressive and innately driven to dominate their peers. Macho cultures also value tolerance of harsh treatment, because it is assumed as indicative of strength and maturity, and include the belief that "homosexual involvement" is deviant (Hartill 2005, 2009; Mendel 1995).

Men and boys embedded in macho organizational cultures may be more inclined to perpetrate child sexual abuse. In macho cultures, men and boys who sexually abuse children may view themselves as simply acting out their innate and desirable aggressive tendencies. Macho cultural content has been linked to boys' sexual abuse of peers, both girls and boys (Green and Masson 2002; Hartill 2009; Parkin and Green 1997). Macho cultural elements may have facilitated an instance of organized adult–child abuse in the Oakland, California (USA), Police Department, where several officers sexually abused a teenager who they knew to be engaged in transactional sex. After preliminary investigations, Oakland Mayor Libby Schaaf attributed the abuse to the police department's "toxic, macho culture" (Associated Press 2016).

Further, boys embedded in macho cultures may be more inclined to withhold information about their own abuse. In macho cultures, boys who are victims of abuse may understand themselves to have been either inappropriately passive or partly responsible for their abuse. Further, when their abuse is at the hands of a man or another boy, boy victims may understand their partial responsibility to be symptomatic of sexual deviance (Green 2001; Hartill 2005; Mendel 1995). Indeed, Hartill (2009) describes an instance in which a male coach perpetrator secured a boy victim's silence by threatening to tell others that the boy was homosexual. Finally, boy victims of abuse may understand their abuse, insofar as it constitutes harsh treatment, to be something that should be stoically and silently endured.

What is more, third-party observers of abuse who are embedded in macho cultures may overlook and/or eschew responding to abuse perpetrated by boys. In macho cultures, third-party observers may consider sexual abuse of peers as just "boys being boys" and thus not worthy of suppression. This appears to have been the case at Geelong Grammar School, where teachers assumed that boys' sexual abuse of peers was natural and beneficial to their development, describing it as "good for the soul" and as "toughen(ing) you up" (McKenzie-Murray 2015). Parent and Bannon (2012) contend that macho cultural elements and their association with abusive behavior may be particularly evident in boys' sports organizations.

Finally, the cultures of some youth-serving organizations may even contain "rape" content, which represents an extension of macho content. Rape cultures feature the assumption that men possess stronger sexual impulses than women. They also feature the belief that men and boys' pursuit of sexual gratification is good, whereas women's submissiveness is virtuous (Butler 1993; Powell 2008). Rape culture elements may facilitate the sexual abuse of girls by men and boys (Pringle 1993). Men and boys embedded in such cultures view the aggressive pursuit of sexual gratification as natural, good, and normative. And the aggressive pursuit of sexual gratification by definition entails the satisfaction of sexual desires without consummate consent on the part of the objects of sexual desire.

Rape culture elements may have facilitated an instance of child sexual abuse at Saint Paul's School, an exclusive college-preparatory boarding school in Concord, New Hampshire (USA). There, students participated in an informal annual ritual in which male students competed with one another to obtain the greatest number of sexual encounters with female classmates. This cultural practice may have conveyed the assumption that girls are sexual objects to be acquired and the belief that it is good to acquire as many of these objects as possible. Such cultural content may have increased the likelihood that some boys' sexually acquisitive encounters with girls would be nonconsensual, as appeared to have been the case in one highly publicized instance (Bidgood 2015).

5.3.2 Cultural Understandings Pertaining to Intimacy between Adults and Children

The cultures of youth-serving organizations also often contain content pertaining to the development of intimate relationships between adults and children. Cultures sometimes feature assumptions that intimate relationships between adults and children are necessary, beliefs that such relationships are good for children, and norms that adults should enact behavioral expressions of such relationships (e.g., touching, hugging, kissing, sharing of confidences). The extent to which cultures feature this content may influence the likelihood that adults will abuse children and the chance that their abuse will go undetected and inadequately addressed in organizations.

The cultures of some youth-serving organizations feature the assumption that intimate relationships and the enactment of behaviors that express these relationships are integral to the fulfillment of staff role expectations (Mones 2014; Parent and Demers 2011;). In some sports clubs it is considered necessary for coaches to have physical contact with athletes, including contact with athletes in various stages of undress (Hartill 2009). For example, in some of the Australian swimming clubs that were the subject of a Royal Commission case study, the coach role appeared to include giving massages to athletes before or after competition (Case Study No. 15). Similarly, in some sports it is considered necessary for coaches to develop intimate psychological relationships with athletes (Cense and Brackenridge 2001). For example, in gymnastics, coaches may think it appropriate to enquire about and even exert control over an athlete's wake time, bed time, diet, and associates, all of which might be thought to affect athletes' ability to conform to the sport's rigorous training regimen. Cultural content supporting intimate relationships between adults and children may be rooted in perceptions of practical necessity. In addition, the cultures of some youth-serving organizations feature the assumption that the development of intimate relationships between adults and children is indicative of exemplary fulfillment of staff role expectations (Colton, Roberts, and Vanstone 2010; Shakeshaft 2004). For example, in childcare centers, supervisors and parents may consider physical displays of affection toward children to be indicative of desirable staff member concern for children.

When the cultures of youth-serving organizations endorse the development of intimate relationships between adult staff and children and the enactment of behavioral expressions of these relationships, it may increase the likelihood that adult staff members who are not aware of their motivation to abuse children will, through developing intimate and affectionate relationships with children and engaging in behaviors that are expressions of such relationships, discover their latent sexual interest in children. It may also increase the likelihood that people who are not motivated to abuse children or a child will develop the motivation to do so. Thus, Cense and Brackenridge (2001: 70–71) contend that the development of intimate relationships between coaches and athletes in sports clubs constitute "athletic risk factors" for child sexual abuse.

Further, when the cultures of youth-serving organizations endorse the development of intimate relationships between adult staff and children and the enactment of behavioral expressions of these relationships, it can undermine the ability of even vigilant organizational members to identify perpetrators of child sexual abuse. Adult child sex abusers often enact intimate relationships with children as part of a self-conscious effort to groom children for abuse. Grooming can consist of a variety of tactics, such as performing favors, providing gifts, and sharing confidences with victims, all of which are designed to gain the trust of victims, victims' guardians, and other possible protectors in the environment, as well as to gauge victims' propensity and ability to resist perpetrators' advances (Conte et al. 1989). When cultures endorse intimate relationships between adults and children, perpetrators' grooming activities may appear normative. This appears to have been the case at the Caringbah OSHC facility described earlier, where Jonathan Lord sexually assaulted twelve children. One of Lord's coworkers, Danielle Ockwell, testified that she saw Lord engaging in behavior that many would consider indicative of grooming. But she did not report his behavior because she did not perceive it to be inappropriate in the OSHC context. Ms. Ockwell testified that she saw a child on Lord's lap for most of the afternoon but did not tell anyone because "She understood that there should not be unnecessary touching between staff and children, but she did not consider that children sitting on laps constituted unnecessary or inappropriate touching" (Case Study No.2, 63).

5.3.3 Cultural Understandings Pertaining to the Sexual Character of Behavior

The cultures of youth-serving organizations also sometimes contain content pertaining to the sexual character of their members' behavior. Cultures sometimes feature norms that authorize sexualized behaviors, that is, behaviors that appear to have unambiguous sexual connotations. For example, the use of gender-stereotyped language, the viewing of advertising and music videos that sexualize women and girls, and the watching of pornography are frequent practices in some youth-serving organizations. Cultures also sometimes feature the assumption that interaction among organizational members is inherently sexual in character – that is, motivated by sexual impulses or designed to convey sexual intentions. For example, in some youth-serving organizations dress, posture, and hugs are interpreted as having sexual connotations. Even the cultures of organizations that provide services to very young children can be sexualized, featuring sexual exploration games such as "doctor," the use of sexual words, and overt reactions such as giggling to hearing such words (Lindblad et al. 1995).

Children who are embedded in sexualized cultures may develop the motivation to pursue sexual relationships with peers, which can be abusive. Some report that sexualized cultures are linked to children's development of sexually harmful behavior (McKibbin, Humphreys, and Hamilton 2015; Timmerman and Schreuder 2014). We suspect that adults who are embedded in sexualized cultures also may develop the motivation to pursue sexual relationships with children, which are by definition abusive. Further, we suspect that third-party observers who are embedded in sexualized cultures, like those embedded in cultures that endorse the development of intimate relationships between adults and children, may find it difficult to distinguish between adult–child interactions that are constituent of grooming and those that are not.

Alternatively, the cultures of youth-serving organizations may feature norms that code all sexualized behaviors as inappropriate and contain the assumption that interaction among members is inherently asexual in character. Cultures that feature such norms and assumptions may fail to endorse the discussion of sex-related matters or even code the discussion of sex-related matters as taboo. When this happens, adults and children may lack knowledge of the distinction between appropriate and inappropriate adult–child interaction. Further, adults may be ill equipped to manage their sexual arousal and children may be ill equipped to resist perpetrators' sexual advances. Keenan (2012) contends that the Catholic Church's tendency to eschew and even discourage the discussion of sex-related matters may have facilitated the child sexual abuse perpetrated by priests that was brought to worldwide attention in the late 1990s. Priests who were not given the opportunity to address sex-related matters had difficulty navigating their commitment to celibacy, which likely ran counter to their biological and socially conditioned sexual desires. Likewise, Catholic children who were not given the opportunity to discuss sex-related matters found it difficult to interpret and resist the sexual abuse perpetrated against them.

Organizational cultures that stifle the discussion of sex-related matters may also impede the detection of abuse and undermine the response to abuse when it is detected. When organizational cultures suppress the discussion of sex-related matters, victims of child sexual abuse may be reluctant to report the abuse because they do not have the language to describe it. Several survivors who were abused at the Winlaton Youth Training Centre in Victoria, Australia, testified that they were given little information about sex-related matters. For example, survivor BHE testified that every time she was sent back to Winlaton after running away, she was subjected to sexually transmitted disease examinations, but "was never told why she had to undergo these checks" (Case Study No. 30, 62). Thus, it is no surprise that some of the Winlaton women survivors testified that they had difficulty understanding the child sexual abuse perpetrated against them, and had trouble conveying information about the abuse to others. For example, BHE testified that the abuse she experienced at the hands of a social worker left her feeling "confused" (Case Study No. 30, 62). Another survivor, BDC, testified that she did not report the abuse perpetrated against her by other children because she "didn't know what to say or how to say it" (Case Study No. 30, 62).

Finally, when organizational cultures stifle the discussion of sex-related matters, third-party observers may be slow to react to signs of abuse that they observe. Signs of abuse, especially grooming, are frequently ambiguous. When organizational cultures endorse the discussion of sex-related matters, third-party observers of ambiguous signs of abuse can consult with superiors, peers, and subordinates to evaluate their perceptions of potential sexual abuse. But when organizational cultures stifle discussions of sex-related matters, people who witness ambiguous signs of abuse are likely to keep their thoughts to themselves. This tendency has been noted in connection with child sexual abuse perpetrated in sports clubs (Parent and Bannon 2012).

5.3.4   Cultural Understandings Pertaining to Violence

The cultures of youth-serving organizations may also contain content pertaining to the use of violence by adults against children, where violence is here taken to mean the use of psychological pressure and physical force that sometimes are understood to constitute psychological and physical abuse. Specifically, cultures may variably feature the assumptions that children are intractable and even dangerous, and that psychological pressure and physical force are effective means of instruction and control for intractable and dangerous children. Together these two assumptions can form the basis of a penal frame of reference. The use of psychological pressure and physical force that can constitute abuse may have its roots in more general cultural content pertaining to the use of violence. Parkin and Green (1997) report that the managers of some group homes treat staff in a psychologically and physically abusive fashion. Further, they contend that this leads workers to treat children in their care abusively, which in turn leads children to treat one another abusively. A number of well-researched social psychological processes might underpin the tendency of those who are abused to abuse others, including social learning (Bandura 1963) and social comparison theory (Festinger 1954).

Adult use of psychological pressure and physical force against children can lead to the perpetration of sexual abuse. Statistical evidence indicates that psychological, physical, and sexual abuse often co-occur (Finkelhor, Ormrod, and Turner 2007; Goldsworthy 2015). Anecdotal evidence indicates that physical abuse and sexual abuse are sometimes enacted as two components of a single strategy to denigrate and punish people (Hersh 2004a). Finally, it seems possible that psychological and physical abuse can evolve into sexual abuse. When a person treats another person unethically, they become desensitized to the guilt that accompanies the pursuit of unethical behavior and they relax the ethical benchmark they use to evaluate their behavior, making them psychologically and cognitively prepared to engage in repeated and increasingly unethical behavior (Ashforth and Anand 2003; Palmer 2008). Thus, when adults psychologically and physically abuse a child, they may become psychologically and cognitively prepared to sexually abuse them in the future.

5.3.5 Cultural Understandings of Childhood and Children

The cultures of youth-serving organizations often contain content pertaining to whether young people should be considered children. When the cultures of youth-serving organizations feature the assumption that young people are not children, staff members and even children may be more inclined to consider sexual relationships between adults and children as acceptable. A report on USA Swimming's sexual abuse prevention policies concluded that swimming officials' propensity to refer to young people as "athletes" rather than as "children" fostered an environment in which romantic relationships between coaches and their young swimmers were condoned (Evans, Alesia, and Kwiatkowski 2016; Hobson and Rich 2017).

The cultures of youth-serving organizations also contain content pertaining to the characteristics of persons categorized as children. Importantly, cultures often contain content pertaining to the trustworthiness of children. When the cultures of youth-serving organizations feature the assumption that children are untrustworthy, staff members may be less likely to believe the reports of children who are victims or third-party observers of child sexual abuse. Further, children who are victims or third-party observers will be less likely to come forward to disclose the abuse they experience or observe because they doubt they will be believed. Children may be reluctant to report abuse if they expect their reports will be disbelieved because they have little to gain from reporting the abuse, and may in fact expose themselves to the risk of retaliation by the abuser and their allies as well as rejection by their peers. The tendency of children's reports of abuse to be ignored has been observed in schools, where the denials of teachers who have sexually abused children are more likely to be believed than the disclosures of the students who have been abused (Shakeshaft 2004; Shakeshaft and Cohen 1994). The possibility of reprisals for revealing abuse manifested at the Geelong Grammar School, where a student who reported abuse perpetrated by a staff member was expelled from the school after discussing the abuse with a peer despite admonishments to remain silent (Case Study No. 32, 14).

The cultures of youth-serving organizations also often contain content pertaining to the extent to which children should enjoy unrestricted opportunities to speak with other children or adults, especially about matters that might cast adults in a negative light. When the cultures of youth-serving organizations do not support the norm that children should speak freely to other children or adults, children who are victims or third-party observers of child sexual abuse will be less able to disclose the abuse. This was the case at the Parramatta Training School for Girls and the Institution for Girls in Hay in New South Wales, Australia. At Hay, girls were prohibited from speaking with one another for more than ten minutes a day, were required to stay at least six feet apart from each other when in public areas, and were instructed to keep their heads down when walking around the grounds so they could not easily take note of peers in their vicinity. More subtly, several abuse survivors of Parramatta and Hay told the Royal Commission that residents were commanded to speak with staff only when spoken to. Thus, as one survivor testified, unless a staff member asked an inmate whether she had been abused, she could not disclose the abuse (Case Study No. 7, 13).

5.3.6 Cultural Content as a Resource

The preceding discussion assumes that an organization's members reflexively adopt its cultural content by virtue of their membership in the organization. But organizational members, especially powerful members, can use cultural content as a resource to pursue their interests. And when powerful organizational members are predisposed to abuse children, they can use cultural content to follow through on this predisposition.

Persons who are predisposed to abuse children can draw on cultural content in the organization or its environment to facilitate their abuse of children. For example, adults predisposed to abuse children may intentionally expose children in their care to pornographic material, observe whether they react with interest or disgust to the material, and then decide whether to pursue abuse of the children based on their reaction to pornography (Colton, Roberts, and Vanstone 2010; Conte et al. 1989; Moulden et al. 2010).

Further, persons engaged in the abuse can use cultural content in the organization to impede detection. Steven Larkins, chief executive officer of the Hunter Aboriginal Children's Services OSHC in New South Wales, Australia, appears to have drawn on cultural content from the Aboriginal community to inhibit the detection of child abuse in which he was engaged. Larkins encouraged staff and board members of the Hunter OSHC to view the Australian government agencies charged with monitoring them, which were not staffed by Aboriginal peoples, as illegitimate watchdogs (Menzies and Stoker 2015).

In addition, persons who have abused children can use cultural content in the organization to undermine their organization's or external agencies' response. Catholic Church officials considered child sexual abuse to be a sin, which in church doctrine could be forgiven. Further, they understood child sexual abuse as emanating from a frailty of the soul, which could be healed. These cultural assumptions were used to justify the internal investigation and adjudication of child sexual abuse cases (following Church canon law), and the internal rehabilitation of abusers (in specialized Church affiliated treatment facilities), in lieu of their referral to external legal authorities that were likely to respond more effectively to the abuse (Boston Globe 2002).

Persons predisposed to abuse children can even manufacture cultural content to facilitate their abuse of children, impede detection of their abuse, and undermine response to their abuse. For example, some maintain that Frank Beck, the officer-in-charge of three Leicestershire County Council (UK) children's homes, developed a therapeutic model for treating children with behavioral problems that provided a "cover" for his and his staff's abuse of children in their care (D'Arcy and Gosling 1998). Beck's model entailed returning children to a state of infancy, a version of "regression therapy," under the presumption that doing so would surface emotional disturbances that were the root of the children's behavioral problems so that the underlying emotional disturbances could be addressed and manifested behavioral problems resolved. One element of Beck's model called for staff to come into contact with children in various stages of undress, as was the case when staff clothed children in diapers or administered baths to them. This characterization of Beck's steward-ship of the Leicestershire County Council children's homes, though, has been contested (Webster 1999). Similarly, some maintain that caregivers in day care centers manufactured cultural content (e.g., satanic beliefs) and practices (e.g., satanic rituals) to facilitate the abuse of children in the 1980s (Finkelhor 1988). This assertion, though, also has been contested (de Young 2004).

6 Institutional Processes

Finally, formal organizations also coordinate organizational participant beha-vior through institutional structures. Theorists who study these structures conceptualize them very broadly, so broadly as to incorporate many of the structural elements already discussed earlier. In this section we consider only those institutional structures (and associated processes) that do not overlap with the structural elements already discussed and that are germane to child sexual abuse.[8]

6.1   Bureaucratic Morality: An Oxymoron

Max Weber, the progenitor of institutional thought in sociology, characterized formal organizations, especially those that conform to the bureaucratic model, as devices for transforming substantive problems into technical ones. Indicative of this, he concluded his classic analysis of the cultural foundations of capitalism by likening the bureaucratic form to an "iron cage" (Weber 2011). In transforming substantive problems into technical ones, formal organizations diminish organizational participants' feeling of moral responsibility for their actions. Formal organizations use hierarchical and horizontal divisions of labor, which compartmentalize organizational participants' responsibilities. They also use rules and standard operating procedures, which specify how participants are to fulfill their responsibilities. As a result, participants focus only on a subset of tasks and the specified ways to accomplish those tasks, rather than on the merits (including the moral merits) of these tasks and their outcomes. This tendency has been identified as a hallmark of the modern

---

[8] For more assessment of the role that institutional structures play in organizational misconduct more generally, see Palmer (2017).

corporation (Jackall 1988). It has also been considered a root cause of organizational misconduct ranging from the Holocaust (Bauman 2001) to child sexual abuse in the Catholic Church (Hinings and Mauws 2006).

The fundamental tendency of formal organizations to transform substantive problems into technical ones likely inhibits the detection of child sexual abuse in organizational contexts. Members of formal organizations may overlook indications that child sexual abuse is occurring because the detection of child sexual abuse is not their assigned responsibility. This tendency was evident in the Caringbah OSHC facility, where Jonathan Lord sexually abused twelve children. The authors of the Royal Commission study of the abuse concluded that Caringbah's staff did not exhibit "shared personal responsibility to keep children safe" (Case Study No. 2: 72).

The fundamental tendency of formal organizations to transform substantive problems into technical ones also likely undermines response to detected abuse. This tendency was evident in the Catholic Education Office's (CEO) response to allegations of child sexual abuse at Saint Ann's Special School in Adelaide, Australia. As the "coordinator of resources" for the CEO, Michael Critchley was responsible for overseeing St. Ann's and other Catholic schools in the region, and he followed the organization's policies and procedures to the letter when he was informed of the abuse. Rather than notify his superiors at the CEO of the abuse and immediately commence a special investigation of the matter, which might have generated a swifter and more effective response, Critchley addressed the matter himself as if it was a routine human resources management issue. As he testified in 2014, Critchley wished that he had enquired further about the problem and notified the CEO director immediately. Further, he "could think of no real or perceived barriers that prevented him from taking those steps" (Case Study No. 9: 23). Critchley's failure to more adequately respond to the abuse was at least partly due to the fact he was simply following rules. Indeed, an investigation of the Education Office concluded that Critchley "responded to the allegations of sexual abuse in accordance with his duties and responsibilities in accordance with accepted expectations and procedures relating to reports of child sexual abuse as they existed at the time" (23).

6.2 The Institutional Functions of Top Management

Weber's institutional insights were developed into an analytic framework now known as the "old institutionalism" that provided an important cornerstone of modern organizational theory (Parsons 1956a, 1956b: Selznick 1948). Proponents of the old institutionalism maintained that the highest levels of any organization are chiefly responsible for managing the organization's relation-ships with external stakeholders that provide the organization with resources and legitimacy (Pfeffer 1976). Most important, senior officials are tasked with ensuring that their organization is insulated from external threats such as adverse publicity and legal action. In the case of private sector enterprises, leaders are legally required to pursue this mandate in the interests of shareholders. In the case of nonprofit organizations, leaders answer to a variety of constituencies that might expect them to pursue this mandate, including rank-and-file members, alumni, governing boards, financial supporters, and funding bodies. Leaders who undergo professional training, such as those who pursue advanced degrees in business, public, and nonprofit administration, often learn skills to manage negative publicity and legal challenges. Thus, it is likely that leaders prioritize protecting the organization's public image and reducing its exposure to legal challenges, even at the expense of protecting the interests of workers, clients, and other organizational stakeholders.

Youth-serving organizations can experience severe negative consequences from disclosures of child sexual abuse. The prosperity and survival of such organizations hinge on their reputation as safe and nurturing environments for children. High-profile cases of child sexual abuse undermine that reputation. The Boston Catholic Archdiocese's impressive financial resources were sig-nificantly depleted in the wake of large civil suit judgments (Ruhl and Ruhl 2015). Thus, while reprehensible, organizational leaders tend to respond to disclosures of child sexual abuse in ways that minimize scandal and adverse legal judgments, but sacrifice the welfare and rights of victims. This tendency is accentuated in large organizations that can afford to keep crisis management experts on staff, or that can afford to hire such experts when child sexual abuse occurs. Crisis management experts are professionally bound to defend their clients against claims of responsibility for child sexual abuse, even when they know their client is guilty. This tendency reaches its objective apex (and moral nadir) when an organization retains or contracts with lawyers to fulfill or aid in the crisis management function. Lawyers operate within an adversarial system, in which they are bound to use the most aggressive tactics in defense of their clients, including attacking the veracity and integrity of victims and their supporters.

The tendency of organizational leaders to react to disclosures of child sexual abuse as threats to manage rather than as problems to address was evident at Geelong Grammar School. When the head of the school's Glamorgan campus, Phillipa Beeson, became aware of the abuse perpetrated by a teacher (BIM), her main concern appears to have been the threat that disclosure of the abuse posed for the school, rather than the harm caused to the victim (BIR). Following revelation of the abuse, Ms. Beeson wrote a note in which she stated that she contacted Ivan Sutherland, the prior head of Glamorgan campus who hired the abuser. In that note, she wrote that Mr. Sutherland acknowledged that he knew the teacher had a prior history of abuse when he hired him and that her "nightmare is knowing about [the teacher] BIM, Ivan still let him take boys on a *REDACTED* weekend. If [the student] BIR get[s] wind of this, we could have a real problem on our hands" (Case Study No. 32: 20). The tendency of organizational leaders to defend their organizations against allocations of child sexual abuse by attacking victims and their supporters was evinced in the Boy Scouts of America's response to allegations of child abuse directed at scout masters, which included dogged attempts to discredit and intimidate the abused children and their parents (Boyle 1994).

6.3 Institutionalized Organizations

Proponents of old institutionalism also maintain that organizational partici-
pants sometimes come to view their organizations as ends in themselves, independent of the goals they were established to pursue. When this occurs, the organizations are said to have become "institutionalized," and to have taken on the character of "institutions" (Clark 1970; Selznick 1949). When organizations become institutionalized, their members view criticisms of the organiza-
tion as unjust and consider defense against the criticisms to be of paramount importance. This is because the psychological identities of organizational participants (i.e., how organizational participants see themselves) tend to fuse with the identity of their organization (i.e., the organization's values). When this happens, organizational participants view an effective response to threats facing the organization as one that protects their own identity (Vadera and Pratt 2016). Organizational leaders may exploit this fusing of organizational and individual identities by threatening those who lobby for truly effective responses to organizational problems with the prospect of expulsion from the organization.

When allegations of child sexual abuse surface in institutionalized organizations, organizational participants tend to question the allegations and see them as threats to be managed in ways that minimize their negative effects on the organization's image. The Catholic Church's response to the child sexual abuse scandal at the turn of this century appears to have followed this pattern. Members of the clergy viewed allegations of abuse to be overblown (Archdiocese of Boston 2002; Kay 2002) and they withheld information about sexual abuse perpetrated by priests to safeguard the image of the Church (Bartunek 2006; Keenan 2012). The Mormon Church's response to individual instances of child sexual abuse appears to follow the same pattern. Church leaders encouraged victims and adult survivors of abuse who came forward to "forgive the church" so as not to "disturb the image of church leaders as benevolent protectors." Further, Church leaders threatened to ban victims and survivors who were not persuaded by this argument from public praying or speaking, referred to as "disfellowship" (Gerdes et al. 1996).

While the old institutionalism did not explicitly maintain it, we suspect that entire organizational fields also can be institutionalized. Thus, Hartill (2013) contends that in male sports organizations, members exhibit a "double consciousness," which essentially leads them to overlook abuse they may observe. In Hartill's words: "The field of sport persistently represents itself ... as a philanthropic force, simply providing healthy, fun, positive opportunities for children to interact, learn, and develop" (2013: 249). To acknowledge child sexual abuse in this domain threatens to undermine the belief that sport is an unmitigated positive force in children's lives.

6.4   Formal Organizations as Myth and Ceremony

A variant of institutional theory, which has variably been referred to as "new institutional theory," "neo-institutional theory," and the "new institutionalism," emerged in the late 1970s and became the dominant form of organizational theorizing in the final years of the twentieth century (Scott 1987, 2008). While this approach partly represents a synthesis of insights from Weber, the "old institutionalism" of Selznick and Parsons, and other modern theories of organizations, including theories pertaining to culture, administrative systems, and power structures, it offers some significant new insights into the functioning of organizations (Palmer, Biggart, and Dick 2008). The first statement of the new institutional approach characterized organizations as "myth and ceremony," the myth being the belief that organizations are rational and the ceremony being practices that foster this belief. It also characterized organizations as "loosely coupled systems," in which the myth and ceremonies that organizations embrace diverge from the actual processes through which organizations carry out their business. For example, new institutional theorists portray schools as fostering the myth that they are rational systems for educating students, and as conducting ceremonies like the writing of lesson plans and the dissemination of student evaluation forms, neither of which plays a significant role in the actual teaching of students (Meyer and Rowan 1977).

While the above characterization might be an exaggeration, it is a useful corrective to the view that organizations are fully rational systems. Formal organizations employ impersonal divisions of labor, policies and procedures, and rules, all designed with the apparent intent to efficiently and effectively achieve stated goals. Some of an organization's division of labor, policies and procedures, and rules pertain to the selection, socialization, monitoring, and rewarding and punishing of organizational members. But these administrative systems are sometimes more window dressing than operative. In short, people inside and outside of an organization may trust that an organization is operating rationally, when in fact it is not. And this exposes children to heightened risk of sexual abuse.

Specifically, parents tend to assume that staff members of youth-serving organizations have been subjected to careful screening, training, and monitoring. As a result, parents tend to entrust the care of their children to the staff of youth-serving organizations without feeling the need to independently screen and monitor these staff persons. Further, parents are likely to employ the staff of youth-serving organizations as independent childcare providers without feeling the need to conduct independent due diligence. Thus, generally speaking, formal organizations provide cover for persons who are predisposed to abuse children. The blind trust afforded the staff of youth-serving organizations appears to have facilitated Jonathan Lord's abuse of children at the Caringbah OSHC. While all of the abused children were enrolled in the Caringbah OSHC, most were abused in their own homes, where Lord was employed as a child-sitter.

New institutional theorists have devoted a considerable amount of attention to explaining the origins and proliferation of organizational practices, ceremonial and otherwise, through organizational fields. The first and most influential explanation attributes the creation and spread of organizational practices to three processes: mimicry, or the copying of other organizations' practices; normative pressures, or the adoption of officially authorized practices; and coercion or conformity to the requirements of dominant actors in the field (DiMaggio and Powell 1983). We strongly suspect that administrative systems purportedly designed to improve detection and enhance response to child sexual abuse arise and spread through these same institutional processes, such that the nature of these administrative systems varies across the different youth-serving organization fields (e.g., childcare centers, sports organizations, youth prisons) but exhibits homogeneity within fields.

6.5 The Professions and Organized Religions as Legitimating Entities

Recently, an even newer variant of institutional theory has been advanced. This variant, the institutional logics perspective, holds that institutions vary according to their "logics," which roughly speaking, consist of principles according to which the social world is assumed to operate (Thornton, Ocasio, and Lounsbury 2012). The progenitors of this perspective identify seven ideal typical logics, three of which may serve to facilitate child sexual abuse, impede detection of abuse, and undermine response to abuse. We have already discussed one of the three logics, the bureaucratic logic, earlier. Here we discuss the other two, professional and religious logics.

Professions, such as medicine, the law, and education, are a subset of occupations that share several defining characteristics, two of which are particularly important from the standpoint of child sexual abuse. First, professionals are obligated to act in the best interest of those they serve (e.g., patients, criminal defendants, students), rather than in their self-interest. Second, professionals are monitored by groups of their peers to ensure that they fulfill their obligations to those they serve. For this reason, outsiders tend to view professionals as trustworthy and allow them access to children unsupervised. Thus, professions also provide cover for persons who are predisposed to or develop the disposition to abuse children. This is likely one reason why Dr. Larry Nassar was afforded unsupervised contact with the young athletes whom he abused and one reason why the young athletes tolerated his abusive behavior, which he represented as medically necessary. It is also likely one reason why he was able to rebuff early allegations of abuse. It was only after multiple victims came forward that Dr. Nassar's representations of his behavior were doubted (Hobson 2017).

Religions tend to embrace beliefs that place a high value on benevolence toward others. For this reason, both members and nonmembers of religious organizations tend to view officials of organized religions as trustworthy and allow them unsupervised access to children. Thus, organized religions also provide cover for persons who are predisposed to abuse children. This is likely one reason why Catholic priests were afforded unsupervised contact with the children whom they abused, one reason why children complied with priests' abusive advances, and one reason why priests were able to rebuff allegations of abuse for so long (Boston Globe 2000).

6.6 The Normalization of Misconduct

Finally, a number of theorists have developed an understanding of how misconduct can become institutionalized, that is, redefined as normal and embedded in standard operating procedures. Diane Vaughan (1996) was the first and remains the foremost of these theorists. In her analysis of the Space Shuttle Challenger disaster, she found that pragmatic political and economic exigencies led the National Aeronautic and Space Administration (NASA) to set tight launch schedules, which in turn caused NASA contractors to deviate in small ways from established safe practice. Further, when those deviations did not produce significant negative consequences in the short run, they were incorporated in the contractors' standard operating procedures. Moreover, as standard operating procedures were adjusted to allow for deviations from established safe practice, the culture of NASA began to shift. Whereas early in the manned space program's history, decision-makers operated under the assumption that launches should only proceed if engineers could prove that systems were safe, decision-makers increasingly came to operate under the assumption that launches should only be delayed or canceled if engineers could prove that systems were unsafe. In Vaughan's terminology, the deviant behavior became "normalized." Eventually, the deviations from established safe practice and the shifting culture led to the catastrophic failure of the Challenger's solid rocket boosters, the destruction of the shuttle, and the loss of its crew.

We think the process through which deviant behavior can be normalized in organizations can facilitate child sexual abuse in youth-serving organizations. Specifically, we think that practical exigencies such as resource constraints and effectiveness considerations can lead senior staff of youth-serving organizations to deviate from established child-safe policies.[9] And when those deviations do not lead to detected instances of child sexual abuse, they can become incorporated into standard operating procedures and ultimately find support in assumptions, values and beliefs, and norms that come to populate the organization's culture. Specifically, it may become assumed that child-safe policies are ineffective, flexible departure from such policies may become valued, and conformity to specific workarounds may become the norm. And when new staff members are hired, they may be socialized into these views and trained how to implement the workarounds.

For example, child-safe organization guidelines typically call for rigorous screening of job applicants, but employee and volunteer turnover in youth-serving organizations tends to be high and unpredictable. As a result, these organizations often find themselves searching for new staff on short notice, which may cause staff to depart from established screening procedures. This may explain why Jacqui Barnat, the children's services manager for the southern region of YMCA NSW, failed to subject Jonathan Lord, an applicant for a job at the Caringbah OSHC facility, to a thorough background check. Barnat urgently needed to fill a vacancy at the Caringbah facility and she hired Lord to fill the vacancy because he was the son of a former Caringbah OSHC employee

---

[9] Child-safe policies primarily focus on incentive systems, administrative systems, and cultural arrangements believed to inhibit the perpetration of child sexual abuse, speed the detection of abuse, and enhance the response to abuse (Tucci et al. 2015).

and was referred to her by two current YMCA NSW staff members, presumably reasoning that these informal references were an adequate substitute for a more time-consuming formal screening process. As noted earlier, this substitute recruitment process failed to unearth the fact that Lord had been dismissed from a previous YMCA camp post because he was suspected of abusing a young camper. And within two years, Lord was suspected of sexually abusing several children at Caringbah (Royal Commission Case Study No. 2).

We also think that behaviors that constitute grooming and less invasive forms of abuse can be normalized in organizations. For example, some contend that sexual abuse can be portrayed as acceptable and even expected in sports organizations, where close psychological and physical relationships between coaches and athletes occur on a regular basis and are viewed as inherent to the athletic training enterprise. For example, Parent writes, "Given the particular culture of some sports, athletes may normalize inappropriate behaviors and therefore not perceive sexual abuse by the coach as inappropriate" (2011: 323).

In fact, we think that even behaviors that constitute the most egregious forms of child sexual abuse can become normalized as an inherent part of organizational life, even if the abuse is not explicitly framed as a valued and appropriate behavior. Parkin and Green (1997) provide quotes from former residents of a group home to this effect. For example, they quote one former resident as stating:

> I've seen a girl raped when all of the other kids were holding the door shut and she was being called frigid. I've known girls since [who] talk about being forced into sex they didn't want. And if you were outside a kids' home that would be rape but in a kids' home it is just seen as par for the course.
>
> (1997: 84)

7 Total Institutions

We have analyzed how five building blocks of formal organizations can facilitate child sexual abuse, impede detection of abuse, and undermine response to abuse. In this section, we consider whether particular types of organizations possess unique risks in relation to the perpetration, detection, and response to abuse. Considering the types of organizations that pose unique risks in relation to child sexual abuse has mostly been the province of public health scholars who have employed correlational analyses to identify organizational "risk factors" associated with the occurrence of abuse, the slow detection of abuse, and inadequate response to abuse (cf. Kaufman and Erooga 2016). In contrast, we take a theoretical approach to the problem.

There are two theoretical paths we could take. We could draw on our analysis of how organizational structures influence the perpetration, detection, and response to child sexual abuse and develop an abstract typology of organizations that vary according to their risks in relation to abuse. Alternatively, we could consider types of organizations that are already known to organization theorists and, drawing on our analysis of how organizational features influence the perpetration, detection, and response to child sexual abuse, identify the types that possess unique risks. We pursue the second approach, because the first can generate classifications of organization that have few empirical referents. Specifically, we focus on a type of organization that is well represented on the organizational landscape, that has received significant attention from organizational theorists, and that we think presents unique risks in regard to child sexual abuse: *total institutions*.

The literature on child sexual abuse in organizations sometimes notes the problematic aspects of total institutions in regard to child sexual abuse (cf. Keenan 2012: 50–51). But the analysis of total institutions in this literature remains undeveloped, focusing primarily on the tendency of total institutions to foster antithetical relationships between staff and inmates and, to a greater extent, the tendency of these institutions to promote secrecy. In the following we present a more comprehensive analysis of the ways in which total institutions pose unique risks with respect and particular challenges in regard to detection and response to child abuse.

7.1 The Characteristics of Total Institutions

Erving Goffman (1961) presented the definitive analysis of total institutions, which he maintained had four defining characteristics. First, members are sharply subdivided into a large managed group, referred to as "inmates," and a small supervisory staff. Second, inmates are physically and socially isolated from civil society. Third, the supervisory staff controls inmates' lives in a comprehensive manner that effectively dissolves the separation between inmates' work and personal identities. Fourth, the organization's overarching purpose is the transformation of inmates from a socially undesirable state to a socially desirable one. In Goffman's words, all total institutions are "forcing houses for changing persons; each is a natural experiment on what can be done to the self" (1961: 12). Goffman classified total institutions into five subtypes based on their specific purpose: organizations that care for harmless individuals (e.g., foster homes), organizations that heal purportedly harmful individuals (e.g., psychiatric hospitals), organizations that protect society from purportedly harmful individuals (e.g., prisons), organizations that pursue work-like objectives (e.g., boarding schools), and organizations that pursue religious goals (e.g., monasteries).[10]

Goffman understood total institutions to be a Weberian "ideal type." Thus, Goffman offered the caveat at the beginning of his analysis, that "none of the elements I will describe seems peculiar to total institutions, and none seems to be shared by every one of them" (1961: 5). Some organizations conform closely to the total institution ideal type. The juvenile detention facilities and youth prisons that were the subject of Royal Commission case studies, such as the Victorian State-Run Youth Training and Reception Centres at Turana, Winlaton, and Baltara as well as the Parramatta Training School for Girls and the Institution for Girls in Hay, fall into this category. Other organizations conform more loosely to the total institution ideal type. The Catholic Church, for example, resembles a total institution in several important respects. Persons in training to become priests spend several years in cloisters that are among Goffman's fifth type of total institution, organizations that pursue religious goals (1961: 5). Additionally, a considerable number of priests live on, and the vast majority of priests exclusively work on, Church property after their ordination. Moreover, Church officials tightly regulate priests' dress and appearance, personal property, work assignments, and interpersonal relationships (in particular, sexual relationships) in accordance with Church doctrine and the Code of Canon Law. Finally, a large number of organizations, such as residential grammar schools, exhibit a smaller subset of total institution characteristics (e.g., physical and social isolation from the outside world).

It may be that the number of organizations that conform closely to the total institution ideal type has declined over time. Several of the total institutions that are the subject of Royal Commission case studies, such as the Parramatta Training School for Girls and the Institution for Girls in Hay, no longer exist. Further, it appears that youth-serving organizations that conform to the total institution ideal type, such as the Catholic Church, are increasingly losing their exemptions from mandatory sexual abuse reporting requirements and are coming under increasing external scrutiny. Still, some of the total institutions that were the subject of Royal Commission studies in Australia, such as the Don Dale children's prison, remain in operation today. Further, a new form of total

---

[10] Goffman (1961) acknowledged that the inmates in total institutions have limited domains in which they can exert control over their lives. For example, they sometimes act as if they have changed (that is, they perform as one might in a theatrical production) rather than actually change in ways the institution wants, and sometimes collaborate in their own control. Scott (2010) has developed this acknowledgment into a critique of Goffman's analysis of the total institutional ideal type and used this critique as the basis of her analysis of another emerging ideal type of organization that she dubs the "reinventive institution."

institution is now proliferating throughout the modern world, the refugee camp (de la Chaux, Haugh, and Greenwood 2017).

7.2 The Unique Risks of Total Institutions for Child Sexual Abuse

7.2.1 Total Institutions Promote Secrecy

The physical and social isolation of inmates from civil society is associated with a tendency to limit the flow of information within total institutions (i.e., between senior staff, junior staff, and inmates) and between total institutions and outside entities. The literature on child sexual abuse in organizations has noted this tendency and analyzed its implications in general terms (Green 2001; Wurtele 2012).

We elaborate this tendency in more specific terms. First, the staff members of total institutions tend to withhold information about their organizations' operations from the larger society, so as to buffer themselves from the potential interference of external entities. For example, correctional facilities tightly regulate contact between prisoners and their friends and families. Indeed, total institutions sometimes obtain exemptions from legal requirements pertaining to the release of information to civil society. Catholic Church leaders relied on their exemption from reporting known instances of child sexual abuse to local authorities throughout the twentieth century, preserving for themselves the autonomy to dispose of known abusers as they saw fit. As late as 2013, religious clergy in the United States were exempted from mandatory sex abuse reporting requirements imposed on other persons working with children (for example, teachers, social workers, and healthcare professionals) in twenty-two out of fifty states (Goldenberg 2013).

Second, staff members tend to withhold information from inmates in order to facilitate their control of inmates' attitudes and behaviors. As noted earlier and discussed in more detail in the following, total institutions control inmates' lives in a comprehensive fashion. Inmates are less able to resist staff efforts to control them if they lack information about staff members' intentions. Several survivors giving evidence about their experiences in the Victorian State-Run Youth Training and Reception Centers testified to the opacity of these institutions. For example, they stated that on admission they were strip-searched, given institutional clothing, and placed in holding cells upon induction, all without explanation. Similarly, several survivors reported being subject to intrusive medical examinations without receiving an explanation for the procedure (Case Study No. 30: 58–60). This feature of total institutions likely increases the capacity of persons who are predisposed to abuse children or a specific child to act on that predisposition, by increasing their capacity to circumvent victims' potential resistance.

Third, staff members tend to limit the ability of inmates to communicate with one another. This feature of total institutions restricts the amount of information inmates have about staff intentions and undermines inmates' ability to organize resistance to staff plans. Restrictions on inmate communication with peers were evident at the Institution for Girls in Hay, where residents were prohibited from speaking to each other for more than ten minutes a day, were required to stay six feet away from each other while in public areas, and were instructed to walk with their heads down so they could not take note of peers in their vicinity (Case Study No. 7: 13). This feature of total institutions likely further increases the capacity of persons who are predisposed to abuse children to act on that predisposition by decreasing victims' capacity to obtain advance notice of abusers' intentions and enlist peer support in the face of abusers' advances.

Fourth, senior staff members tend to withhold information from low-level staff. As discussed in detail in the following, total institutions mortify their members' identities, which some staff may consider harsh and even inhumane. Thus, high-level staff members tend to withhold information about their intentions from lower-level staff to obtain their compliance. For example, in military organizations, senior officers only release information to junior officers on a "need to know" basis. This feature of total institutions likely increases the capacity of persons who abuse children to escape detection.

7.2.2   Total Institutions Construct Alternative Moral Universes

The physical and social isolation of inmates from civil society also is associated with a tendency of total institutions to constitute themselves as alternative moral universes. This is particularly evident in military organizations, which maintain their own judicial and prison systems for processing service members believed to have violated military statutes governing appropriate conduct. It is also discernable in boarding schools that have quasi-formalized systems for investigating and adjudicating violations of codes of conduct. When organizations constitute alternative moral universes, it opens up the possibility that these universes are constituted in ways that prioritize the welfare of abuse perpetrators over victims.

For example, the Catholic Church constitutes an alternative moral universe in which priests' behavior is regulated through the application of the Code of Canon Law, a legal system that predates and serves as a model for many contemporary civil society legal systems. Canon law articulates administrative and penal codes and empowers specialized roles for enacting them. Further, members of the Church treat Canon Law as a manifestation of divine inspiration. The Catholic Church's alternative moral universe influenced its response to the piecemeal disclosures of child sexual abuse in the latter half of the twentieth century, which exploded into a public scandal in the first years of the twenty-first century.

Rather than refer alleged perpetrators of sexual abuse to external authorities for investigation, the Church conducted its own investigations and made its own determinations of guilt or innocence of suspects. In addition, rather than turn proven abusers over to civil authorities for sentencing, it handed down its own sentences. In some cases, Church leaders allowed abusers to remain at their posts. In other cases, they transferred abusers to new posts without explanation. In still other cases, Church leaders discreetly enrolled abusers in independent, Church-affiliated or Church-run treatment programs (discussed in detail later), and then reassigned the priests to parish duty when they were deemed rehabilitated (Berry 1992; *The Boston Globe* 2012). Indeed, some Church leaders kept detailed hidden records of offending priests' involvement in abuse and treatment (Boorstein and Zauzmer 2016; Zauzmer 2016). The logic according to which determinations of guilt and the assignment of punishments were established is discussed later in connection with the Catholic Church's theory of human transformation (*The Boston Globe* 2002).[11]

7.2.3 Total Institutions Employ Uniquely Restrictive Formal Authority Structures

The comprehensive control of inmates' lives in total institutions tends to be accomplished via the enactment of uniquely constraining formal authority structures that may influence the perpetration, detection, and response to child sexual abuse. Formal authority relationships between supervisory staff and inmates in total institutions tend to follow a military model. Inmates are expected to take direction from any and all staff members, because all staff members occupy a higher position in the institution's chain of command. This power structure is evident in descriptions of the juvenile detention and residential centers at Parramatta, Hay, Turana, Winlaton, and Baltara. In these institutions, *each* child was required to follow the direction of *any* staff member on a wide range of matters. Indeed, this authority structure is even evident in smaller group foster homes. Parkin and Green (1997) describe a group foster

---

[11] Neustein and Lesher (2008) describe a case in which the Orthodox Jewish community in New York City similarly used an independent judicial apparatus to adjudicate complaints against an alleged perpetrator of child sexual abuse, ultimately vindicating the abuser and stigmatizing the victim and his family.

home whose chain of command followed a model that had military overtones. There, staff members referred to their manager as a "captain running a 'safe ship'" (76–78).

Further, the rewards and punishments that supervisory staff can allocate to inmates in total institutions tend to be extensive, insofar as staff members regulate the conditions of inmates' existence in a comprehensive fashion. Further, the punishments that staff are licensed to administer to inmates tend to be severe, in some cases amounting to psychological and physical abuse. For example, former residents of the Retta Dixon Home in Darwin, Australia, testified that staff members struck residents with a belt until they were cut and bled. In one case, a resident who confronted a host "parent" was stripped of her clothes and bound by chains in a spare room (La Canna 2015). One of the most extreme forms of psychological abuse in these institutions was solitary confinement, which is known to have serious adverse psychological effects (Andersen et al. 2000).

Moreover, the norm of obedience on which supervisory staff in total institutions can rely tends to be comprehensive and strong. Staff can command inmates to engage in, or refrain from, a wide range of behaviors, including when, to whom, and how to speak to staff and fellow inmates. Further, they can expect that inmates will comply with their commands in a consummate fashion. This is evident in descriptions of the detention and residential centers at Parramatta, Hay, Turana, Winlaton, and Baltara, as well as the Retta Dixon Home. In these institutions, children almost always obeyed staff member directives. Comprehensive and strong norms of obedience are even evident in small juvenile residential facilities. Parkin and Green (1997) observed that in the foster home they studied, residents were prohibited from accessing their house's kitchen without staff approval and were fed in a "regimented" fashion (76–78).

As noted earlier, the more power adults possess over children in institutions, the better positioned they are to sexually abuse them. Most directly, staff members can command children to yield to sexual abuse perpetrated against them and to keep the abuse secret. Further, staff members can punish children if they resist sexual abuse or report it. Many former residents at Parramatta and Hay told the Royal Commission that they did not actively resist the sexual abuse perpetrated against them because they felt obliged to follow the direction of the perpetrator, or because they feared the negative consequences of resisting. In testimony delivered to the Royal Commission, a former resident of the Hay Institute for Girls recounted that a member of the supervisory staff "hit her over the head with a set of keys and threw her into (a) dungeon where he forced her to have oral sex" (Case Study No. 7: 20).

More indirectly, staff members in total institutions can command children to engage in, or refrain from, behaviors that make abuse possible and reporting less likely. Several survivors of abuse perpetrated at the Parramatta Training School for Girls and the Institution for Girls in Hay testified to the Royal Commission that staff sedated them or transferred them to solitary confinement to make it easier for staff members to abuse them. Others gave evidence that they were commanded to speak with staff only when spoken to. Thus, as one survivor testified, unless a staff member asked an inmate whether she had been abused, she could not disclose the abuse (Case Study No. 7: 13). Others gave evidence that they were sent to solitary confinement after being abused, depriving them of the opportunity to report the abuse. Still others testified that they were explicitly threatened with punishment if they were to speak up about their sexual abuse; and some reported being punished when they did speak up, where punishment included being placed in solitary confinement and physical abuse.

Formal authority relationships between upper- and lower-level staff in total institutions are also uniquely constraining, an arrangement justified by the need to maintain order over the potentially restive inmates. Authority relationships between senior and junior staff in total institutions tend to adhere closely to the bureaucratic model, in which superiors command subordinates, who in turn command lower-level subordinates, with subordinates taking direction from a single superior. Further, the norm of obedience to authority governing the relationship between upper- and lower-level staff in total institutions is strong, with staff members typically following superiors' directives to the letter.

These features of the formal authority relations between senior and junior staff can inhibit the detection of abuse in total institutions. Many of the perpetrators of abuse at the Parramatta Training School for Girls and the Institution for Girls in Hay were senior officials, including superintendents, deputy superintendents, and acting managers (Case Study No. 7: 17). Several survivors of abuse at these institutions told the Royal Commission they believed that lower-level staff members knew about the sexual abuse perpetrated against them. One survivor reported that when she told a staff member about her experience of sexual abuse, that person said: "I don't know what we can do about it" (Case Study No. 7: 26). The impact of formal authority differentials on third-party reporting of child sexual abuse is also evident in recent reports that American soldiers were ordered to ignore child sexual abuse perpetrated by Afghan police and army troops. While some soldiers followed these orders, others spoke out against the abuse, and some of those who spoke out received career-ending punishments (Gibbons-Neff 2015; Goldstein 2015).

7.2.4   Total Institutions Eradicate Inmates' Pre-institutional Identities

The transformation of inmates from a socially undesirable to a socially desirable state in total institutions proceeds in two steps. In the first step, staff members eradicate inmates' undesirable pre-institutional identities. Goffman refers to the process through which members' pre-institutional identities are eradicated as the "mortification of the self" (1961: 28). Indicative of this total institution imperative, the early proponents of boarding schools saw them as devices to assimilate Native Americans into American society, and embraced the motto "Kill the Indian in order to save the man" (Smith 2004: 90). Goffman based his ideas on extinguishing inmates' pre-institutional identities on Sanford Dornbush's (1955) analysis of the manner in which military academies eradicate cadets' pre-academy selves.

Total institutions eradicate inmates' pre-institutional identities partly by isolating inmates from supports for their old identities. Inmates are prohibited from retaining personal items that remind them of their old identities, from seeking out and forming bonds with peers who could reinforce their old identities, and from interacting with people in their former environment. Thus, on admission to the Parramatta Training School for Girls, girls were shorn of their hair and separated from their personal items. As noted earlier, at Hay, they were required to stay six feet from fellow inmates in public spaces and to keep their heads down when moving about the facility. They also were barred from speaking with fellow inmates for more than ten minutes a day and were allowed only minimal contact with the outside world. In a telling reference, one survivor told the Royal Commission that the rules barring communication among peers were designed to "break the human spirit."

Total institutions also mortify their members' prior identities through rewards and punishments. Inmates are punished for retaining their old identities and rewarded for abandoning them. The extensive use of punishments for even minor rule infractions was evident at the Parramatta Training School for Girls, the Institution for Girls at Hay, and at the Victorian State-Run Youth Training and Reception Centers.

Finally, total institutions eradicate their members' pre-institutional identities by humiliating them. Total institutions can humiliate inmates' pre-institutional identities by exerting control over aspects of inmates' lives over which they previously enjoyed sole control. Thus, the girls at Hay were required to march as they moved around the facility, rather than allowed to walk in their natural gate. Total institutions can also humiliate inmates' pre-institutional identities by assigning them derogatory names. Thus, staff at both Parramatta and Hay frequently called the girls "sluts," "black dogs," and "prostitutes."

Humiliations can also include violations of inmates' sense of self, physically and psychologically. The girls at Parramatta and Hay were subjected to intrusive body searches and invasive medical exams. They were also forced to let staff members read their personal mail, which, importantly, was done for no particular reason (that is, without inmates having done something to provoke these invasions of the self). Again, in a telling reference, one woman who gave testimony to the Royal Commission referred to their treatment at Parramatta as "humiliating" and as leaving them "without pride or self-respect."

The eradication of inmates' pre-institutional identities has consequences for the way staff members perceive inmates and themselves. Staff members come to see inmates as inanimate objects and themselves as controllers of those objects. As noted earlier, when people see others as inanimate objects subject to their control, they see these others as inferior human beings and themselves as superior. And the more people see others as inferior and themselves as superior, the less they feel obliged to respect the rights and needs of those others (Keltner, Gruenfeld, and Anderson 2003: Kipnis 1972; Lee-Chai, Chen, and Chartrand 2001). Thus, the mortification of inmates' pre-institutional identities may place the staff members of total institutions on a process of progressive and incremental boundary violations to psychological and physical abuse, and ultimately sexual abuse. Green (2001) observed this tendency in her investigation of two local authority residential children's homes in the United Kingdom, where "uniformity, control and surveillance [were emphasized] over care," staff became "desensitized to the children's needs and development," and the resulting environment was "conducive to sexual abuse taking place" (2001: 17).

The mortification of inmates' pre-institutional selves also has implications for the way inmates in total institutions perceive themselves and staff members. Inmates come to see themselves as inanimate objects and understand staff to be their controllers. When people see themselves as inanimate objects controlled by others, they come to view themselves as powerless and succumb to abuse meted out by these others (Haney, Banks, and Zimbardo 1973; Zimbardo 2010). Thus, the mortification of inmates' pre-institutional selves may inhibit the victims of sexual abuse from successfully resisting and reporting the abuse.

7.2.5   *Total Institutions Install New Inmate Identities*

In the second phase of the transformation of inmates' identities, staff members encourage inmates to adopt new socially desirable self-concepts. To accomplish this goal, staff members develop or import theories of human transformation that are rooted in assumptions about human nature. Total institutions that hold their members' transformation as their official purpose employ explicit theories of change and embrace explicit assumptions about human nature. For example, psychiatric hospitals that subscribe to the medical model assume their patients are sick and use psychoanalytic techniques in which patients play a passive, rather than a collaborative, role in their own recovery. Total institutions' assumptions about human nature and theories of human transformation may influence the perpetration and detection of child sexual abuse and responses to it in these institutions. But to understand the influence that a total institution's theory and assumptions can have on child sexual abuse, it is necessary to examine that institution's theories and assumptions. We do this briefly for the Catholic Church.

The Catholic Church operates according to an elaborate system of beliefs about the fundamental nature of human beings and the ways that nature can be transformed. This philosophy is expressed in religious doctrine and canon law and based in the assumption that all human beings are by nature sinful. Through confession, penance, and sincere efforts at redemption, humans can be forgiven and obtain salvation. All Catholics, both lay people and religious, take part in the Sacrament of Reconciliation (confession, penance, and absolution). However, priests may experience the sacrament and these values in a more extensive way because their "formation" process, which can take up to fifteen years, includes reconciliation as a fundamental and regular component of training. Moreover, by committing to living a religious life after their ordination, priests continue to take part regularly in the Sacrament of Reconciliation. This likely leads priests to deeply internalize the idea that all human beings are fundamentally flawed, but always capable of redemption.

As noted earlier, Catholic Church leaders often sent priests determined to have abused children to independent, Church-affiliated, and in some cases Church-run facilities for treatment. In many of these facilities, treatment was informed by the latest developments in psychology and psychiatry. But the Church leaders who were ultimately responsible for the abusers' fate viewed child sex abusers as sinners capable of redemption (*The Boston Globe* 2002: 171–76). Pope John Paul II conveyed this understanding in his communiqué following a meeting with visiting US Cardinals and the head of the US Conference of Catholic Bishops (USCCB) on the burgeoning child sexual abuse scandal. The Communiqué stated that the Church's responsibility in regard to the child sexual abuse scandal was to "promote moral teaching about sexual abuse, to recognized the 'power of Christian conversion', and the ability of a sinner to turn back to God" (Formicola 2006; Vatican 2002). Bishop Wilton Gregory, the head of the USCCB, characterized this understanding more succinctly when, after the meeting with the Pope, he explained to a reporter that the Church "doesn't do crime. It does sin" (Rice 2002). Thus, in many cases, Church leaders negotiated for the release and reassignment of child sex abusers to new parishes, even over the opposition of treatment facility professionals. And many of these released and reassigned priests subsequently reoffended.

7.2.6   Total Institutions Incubate Techniques
of Neutralization

Culture content sometimes stipulates extenuating circumstances in which deviant attitudes and behaviors can be considered acceptable. Sykes and Matza (1957) were the first to describe how culturally stipulated extenuating circumstances can endorse deviant attitudes and behaviors. Their study of several youth gangs found, contrary to the dominant theory of the day, that the values and norms of the adolescents engaged in criminal behavior were no different from those of law-abiding citizens. Rather, the adolescents embraced an elaborate set of understandings about when deviant attitudes and behaviors could rightfully be invoked. These understandings, dubbed "techniques of neutralization," immunized the adolescents from the guilt they otherwise might feel after engaging in misconduct. Mary de Young (1988), drawing on Sykes and Matza, analyzed the presence of techniques of neutralization in the publications of three organizations that advocated the decriminalization of adult–child sexual relationships. Ashforth, Anand, and Joshi (2004), building on Sykes and Matza's study, identified six techniques of neutralization that can facilitate misconduct in organizations that we consider here: denial of victim (also referred to as "moral exclusion"); denial of harm; denial of responsibility; social weighting; balancing the ledger; and appeals to higher loyalty.

Many total institutions house inmates who are members of low-status or pariah groups, such as ethnic, racial, and religious minorities (both indigenous and refugee), mentally and physically disabled persons, and law violators, who the supervisory staff is tasked with managing in one way or another. We think that such total institutions will tend to develop cultures that feature the denial of victim, denial of harm, appeal to higher loyalty, social weighting, and balancing the ledger techniques of neutralization. When a total institution's culture features the denial of victim technique of neutralization, it contains the assumption that members of its large managed group are morally inferior and thus are deserving of any harm done to them. Such a culture also includes the assumption that the members of the total institution's large managed group are less than fully human and thus do not fully experience any harm done to them.

When a total institution's culture features the appeal to higher loyalty technique, the members of the supervisory staff believe that their group has higher moral standing than the large managed group, and thus its rights take precedence over the rights of the large managed group. When a total institution's culture features the balancing the ledger technique, it contains the belief that any wrongdoing perpetrated by members of the supervisory staff against members of the large managed group is compensated for by other good deeds the staff does for the managed group. Finally, when a total institution's culture features the social weighting technique, it features two beliefs that apply to the supervisory group. First, members of the supervisory staff believe that any wrongdoing perpetrated by them against the managed group is no worse than the wrongdoing perpetrated by other entities against the managed group. Second, members of the supervisory group believe that external entities that might monitor and punish them for wrongdoing perpetrated against the managed group do not have legitimate standing to do so.

We think that when a total institution's culture features the denial of victim, denial of harm, appeal to higher loyalty, social weighting, and/or balancing the ledger techniques of neutralization, supervisory staff will be immunized against the guilt that they otherwise might feel when they psychologically, physically, and sexually abuse the inmates in their care. As a result, these cultures increase the likelihood that supervisory staff will psychologically, physically, and sexually abuse inmates. The inmates of several of the institutions that were the subject of Royal Commission case studies and that conformed to the total institution ideal type included low-status or pariah group members and the staff of these institutions appeared to consider the inmates morally inferior. For example, the Retta Dixon Home included primarily Aboriginal children among its large managed group (Case Study No 17). Further the Children's Welfare Act 1954 (Vic) officially categorized the children confined to the Turana, Winlaton, Winlaton, and Baltara Youth Training Centres as being admitted to the institutions for reasons of being "exposed to moral danger" and being deemed "likely to lapse into a life of vice and crime" (Case Study No 30:17). Thus, as noted earlier, the staff at both the Parramatta Training School for Girls and the Hay Institution for Girls frequently called the girls in their care "nobodies, sluts, and liars" (Case Study No 7: 5) and "black dogs" and "prostitutes" (Case Study No 7: 16).

8 Implications and Conclusion

8.1 Implications for Practitioners

The child sexual abuse literature has devoted much attention to the development of guidelines that can make youth-serving organizations "child safe." These guidelines primarily focus on incentive systems, administrative systems, and cultural arrangements believed to inhibit the perpetration of child sexual abuse, speed the detection of abuse, and enhance the response to abuse (Tucci et al. 2015). In the following we evaluate these policy prescriptions and evaluate and elaborate additional policy implications that follow from our analysis.

8.1.1 Prevailing Prescriptions

The literature recommends that organizations should institute incentive systems that inhibit child sexual abuse, speed detection, and enhance response to abuse when it occurs. We think this proposal is sensible and that much good can come from adopting it. However, we also think that the implementation of this policy prescription will face significant hurdles.

The orchestration of incentives, whether rewards or punishments, typically requires the expenditure of resources, and youth-serving organizations frequently operate on highly constrained budgets. Many youth-serving organizations, such as juvenile detention facilities, are operated under the auspices of government agencies that exercise tight control over their budgets. Others, such as childcare centers, are situated in the nonprofit sector where the generation of surplus for investment is minimal. Thus, while it may be optimal to design workspaces so that they offer few opportunities for adults to interact with children unsupervised one-on-one, it may prove prohibitively expensive for organizations to acquire new workspaces or remodel existing ones so all workstations are linked by an uninterrupted line of sight.

The literature on child sexual abuse in organizations also recommends that organizations institute administrative systems that inhibit child sexual abuse, speed detection, and enhance response to abuse when it occurs. Most importantly it recommends the installation of rigorous screening protocols to weed out job and volunteer applicants with a history or motivation to abuse children. Further, it advocates that employees and volunteers be trained to comply with these systems and that supervisors be trained to be vigilant in the monitoring and controlling of employees and volunteers to ensure compliance with these systems. We think this proposal also is reasonable and that much good can come from adopting it. But our analysis and organization theory suggest that implementation of this policy prescription may also face obstacles.

Most narrowly, we think that implementation of rigorous screening protocols will produce little reduction in child sexual abuse. Our analysis suggests that many people who abuse children in organizations do not enter the organization with a preexistent motivation to abuse children. Thus, most people who abuse children in organizations do not have a prior conviction for abuse and do not have psychological profiles that are measurably different from those of persons who do not abuse children (Richards 2011). More broadly, we think that the elaboration of robust administrative systems to curb, detect, and respond to abuse may undermine the organization's capacity to accomplish other important goals related to child development. Organization theorists have long recognized that organizations that employ nonroutine technologies, in which the characteristics of inputs are highly variable and understanding of how to process inputs is imprecise, are not suited for mechanistic structures, in which there are many elaborate rules and regulations (Perrow 2014).

Administrative systems are designed to handle routine situations: that is, contingencies that both occur frequently and can be satisfactorily analyzed in advance. When organizations seek to develop standard operating procedures for nonroutine situations, they can produce rules and standard operating procedures that are inappropriate for situations that may arise. Most youth-serving organizations can be considered to employ nonroutine technologies, insofar as children are highly variable and caring for children is an inexact science. The inappropriateness of rules established to suppress child sexual abuse in the Prince George's County public school system in Maryland, USA, is suggested by the observation of a Prince George teacher who was placed on administrative leave for "kissing a first grader on the top of the head after the girl hugged her." Justifying her decision to kiss the student, the teacher asserted that young children expect physical contact and asked, "are you *not* going to hug a 4-year-old who is crying?" (St. George 2017).

The literature on child sexual abuse in organizations also recommends that organizations embrace "child-safe" cultural elements that inhibit child sexual abuse, speed detection, and enhance response to abuse when it occurs. Advice to embrace child-safe cultural elements include calls to promulgate the assumption that child safety is the top priority of every youth-serving organization, the belief that child safety is more important than other youth-serving organization goals, and norms that convey the expectation that members of youth-serving organizations will conform to policies and procedures designed to ensure child safety. The importance of such exhortations should not be underestimated. Many youth-serving organizations place other goals above child safety. For example, USA Swimming has been criticized for embracing the mantra "win medals, grow the sport, improve customer service, and increase visibility," which implicitly deprioritizes child safety (Evans, Alesiz, and Kwiatkowski 2016). Thus, one swimming coach responded to calls for more rigorous child protection policies in the sport by writing:

The statement was made to me that "protecting athletes from sex abuse is a core function of USA Swimming." That is UTTER NONSENSE. The core business of USA Swimming is BUILD, PROMOTE, AND ACHIEVE. The core business of the FAMILY is to keep our children SAFE.

(Hobson and Rich 2017)

With this said, however, the literature does not provide much guidance on how to instill such child-safe cultural elements into youth-serving organizations, apart from recommendations to align incentives and establish administrative systems that support such content. Prescriptive organization theory can be tapped for this purpose. For example, Schein (1985) maintains that leaders can telegraph cultural content in five ways: (1) by the kinds of people they hire and fire; (2) by the kinds of behavior they reward and punish; (3) by the matters on which they focus their attention; (4) by the way they respond to crises; and (5) by the attitudes and behaviors they exhibit.

Translating this prescriptive organizational theory into practice, though, may prove difficult. Most organization theorists recognize that organizational cultures are anchored in organizational environments. For example, Schein (1995) maintains that organizations tend to evolve cultures that offer solutions to the problems they confront in acquiring and processing inputs and in sourcing outputs, whether those outputs are products or services. As a result, organizational cultures tend to exhibit substantial resistance to change. For example, boarding school cultures featuring the assumption that teachers and students are equals and the norm that teachers should develop intimate and affectionate relationships with students may provide a competitive advantage to schools occupying a particular market niche. And eliminating such cultural content in favor of content that endorses a more impersonal relationship between teachers and students may eliminate such boarding schools' competitive advantage.

8.1.2 Beyond Prevailing Prescriptions

To the best of our knowledge, the literature on child sexual abuse in organizations does not offer recommendations on how power and institutional structures should be designed so as to inhibit, speed detection, and enhance response to child sexual abuse in organizations. Our analysis, though, holds implications for how these two other organizational structures might be configured so as to accomplish these goals. For example, our analysis of power structures indicates that unitary chains of command in which subordinates report to a single superior impede detection and response to instances of child sexual abuse. This implies that the leaders of youth-serving organizations would do well to avoid unitary chains of command, opting instead for matrix-like structures in which subordinates report to multiple superiors.

Similarly, our analysis of institutional dynamics indicates that administrative systems implemented to improve child safety can be incrementally dismantled by seemingly sensible modifications of routines to accommodate practical exigencies. This implies that the leaders of youth-serving organizations would do well to resist the tendency to uncritically adjust standard operating procedures on the fly, opting instead for periodic review of deviations from official policy.

Additionally, our analysis indicates that a prevalent ideal type of formal organization, total institutions, presents unique dangers from a child safety standpoint. This implies that organizational leaders should avoid adopting this organizational configuration, at least in its pure form. De la Chaux, Haugh, and Greenwood (2017) indicate how total institutions can be reconfigured to include "respected spaces" and "listening posts," organizational mechanisms that allow a total institution's large managed group greater meaningful participation in the social construction of their institutional lives.

But those seeking to reform power structures and institutional processes that facilitate abuse, impede detection of abuse, and degrade response to abuse are likely to confront the same and additional obstacles confronted by those seeking to reform incentive systems, administrative systems, and organizational cultures. For example, an organization's power structure tends to evolve in conjunction with its critical contingencies, which to some extent are dictated by immutable market forces (Pfeffer and Salancik 1978). Most institutional processes are governed by societal-level structures and processes, which by their very nature are beyond the influence of individual and even organizational actors (Meyer and Rowan 1977). Further, organizations that have adopted the total institution form may find it difficult to reform it. For example, prisons cannot abandon the total institution configuration in its pure form without sacrificing their control of sometimes-dangerous individuals.

8.1.3   A Way Forward

This consideration of policy prescriptions for inhibiting child sexual abuse, speeding the detection of abuse, and enhancing responses to abuse suggests that child sexual abuse in organizations is likely to remain a persistent problem. There are a plethora of organizational structures that can give rise to abuse, impede the detection of abuse, and undermine response to abuse. And each of these structures and processes is rooted in more encompassing systems and thus resistant to targeted manipulation. This, of course, does not absolve the leaders of youth-serving organizations from doing their best to ensure that all of their organizations' structures and processes are as child safe as they can be. But it does suggest that organizational leaders will have to learn to live with structures and processes that can give rise to abuse, impede detection of abuse, and undermine response to abuse.

We think one way to learn to live with these structures is to alert organizational participants to the inherent risks associated with them and to involve organizational participants, especially lower-level participants, in a collaborative learning and continuous quality improvement process. Lower-level employees are in a unique position to understand the child safety risks associated with organizational structures, as they occupy positions closest to where perpetrators and victims are situated. Further, organizational participant participation in the formulation of organizational initiatives builds commitment to those initiatives. One model for involving organizational participants in a collaborative learning and continuous quality improvement process is that used by "high reliability organizations" such as aircraft carriers, where organizational technologies are complex and failure is unacceptable (Weick and Roberts 1993). This model focuses on fostering collaborative environments in which coworkers "heedfully interrelate" across multiple hierarchical levels and horizontal subdivisions in the analysis of "red flags" and "near misses." This model would not only provide organizations with the opportunity to develop flexible means for inhibiting, detecting, and responding to child sexual abuse but would have the likely added benefit of driving out of the organization persons with predispositions to abuse children who would find participation in the continuous quality improvement process distasteful.

8.2   Implications for Organization Theorists

Commentaries on organizational research have distinguished between basic and applied science (Stokes 1997), and between phenomenon and theory-driven enterprises (Davis and Marquis 2005). Our organization theory analysis of child sexual abuse in organizations can be categorized as an applied endeavor, insofar as it is implicitly motivated by a desire to inhibit the perpetration of child sexual abuse, speed detection of abuse, and enhance response to abuse in organizational contexts. It can also be categorized as phenomenon driven, insofar as it is explicitly motivated by the desire to understand child sexual abuse as it occurs in organizations. Further, our analysis can be considered motivated by questions of use and focused on a phenomenon that is relevant to nonmanagerial rather than managerial audiences. It does not appear to constitute a basic science or theory-driven enterprise, insofar as it is not motivated by a desire to test or extend a specific theory or theories about organizations.

Numerous commentators have advocated the pursuit of research such as this (Boulding 1958; Hinings and Greenwood 2002; Nielsen 2018; Pfeffer 2016; Staw 2016; Stern and Barley 1996). Some tout the benefits that it can bring to substantive domains from which it has previously been excluded, enhancing understanding in these domains. Others tout the benefits it can bring to the organization studies community, increasing the perceived "relevance" of the field's activities. Increased relevance to a broad audience can enhance a field's position in the political economy of scholarly pursuits, elevating its status and increasing its perceived worthiness of government research grants and university budget allocations. If our organizational analysis of child sexual abuse in organizational contexts is persuasive, it can extend the footprint of organization theory into the fields of criminology, public health, and social work, and might allow it to capture increased attention and even resources.

One might worry, though, that work such as ours comes at the expense of theory development. Applied and basic science, like theory- and phenomenon-driven work, have long been characterized as mutually exclusive endeavors. But this consensus has recently been called into question. Stokes (1997) maintains that much applied work contributes to basic science understanding. And he cites as an exemplar of this sort of work Pasteur's research on the causes of fermentation and spoilage, which led to the development of the germ theory of disease. Further, Davis and Marquis (2005; Davis 2006) argue that phenomenon-driven research can generate new theory, specifically, middle-range theory that elucidates the mechanisms through which social phenomena can sometimes unfold. And they cite as an exemplar of this sort of work Rogers' (2003) research on the multiple paths through which innovations can diffuse through social networks.

We do not think our organizational analysis of child sexual abuse in organizational contexts surfaces new theory about any of the five organizational structures considered here. But we do think it identifies new ways that these structures can contribute to the perpetration, slow the detection, and undermine the response to misconduct in and by organizations more generally. We highlight three ways in which we believe our work contributes to understandings of organizational misconduct.

First, while theorists have explored how both the characteristics of individuals and organizations contribute to organizational misconduct, they have not considered the relationship between these two determinants of misconduct. We develop a model that identifies three ways in which individual predispositions and organizational membership can interact so as to produce organizational misconduct. Misconduct can arise and flourish within organizations partly through the permeability of organizations to persons with wrongful predispositions, and partly through the propensity of organizations to facilitate organizational participants' discovery of deviant or wrongful predispositions, and partially through the propensity of organizations to facilitate the development of deviant and wrongful predispositions. We think researchers would do well to isolate and investigate these three distinct mechanisms through which misconduct can arise and proliferate in organizations.

Second, we think our analysis of the mechanisms through which organizational structures influence the perpetration, detection, and response to child sexual abuse holds implications for the analysis of ways in which organizational structures might influence the perpetration, detection, and response to other types of misconduct in organizations. While theorists have analyzed in depth the ways in which formal power relationships can facilitate misconduct in organizations, they have devoted relatively little attention to the ways in which informal power can facilitate misconduct. We detail several mechanisms through which informal power relationships can facilitate the perpetration of child sexual abuse and undermine the detection and response to abuse in organizations. And we think that these mechanisms might be invoked to explain how informal power relationships might influence the perpetration, detection, and response to other types of misconduct. Going beyond consideration of formal power relationships to consider informal power relationships is important, because formal power relationships are both simpler (insofar as they tend to operate in a unidirectional fashion) and more transparent (insofar as they are codified in organizational charts and other documents) than informal power relationships

Further, while theorists often attribute misconduct in organizations to cultural arrangements, they seldom dimensionalize culture in a precise fashion, which produces the conflation of culture with other organizational structures. Drawing on Giorgi, Lockwood, and Glynn (2015), we develop a framework for cultural analysis and use this framework to analyze the role that culture plays in child sexual abuse in organizations. And we think this framework can be employed to develop more precise analyses of the role that culture plays in other types of organizational misconduct.

Finally, while institutional theory is the dominant theoretical perspective in organization studies today, its implications for the study of misconduct in organizations has only been explored in a piecemeal fashion. We mine institutional theory to identify a number of institutional mechanisms that influence the perpetration, detection, and response to child sexual abuse in organizations. We think this analysis can inspire analogous analyses of the role that institutional forces play in other types of organizational misconduct.

8.3 Conclusion

In the preceding sections of this Element, we conducted a preliminary organization theory analysis of child sexual abuse occurring in organizational contexts. Specifically, we elaborated how five structures that are fundamental to formal organizations can facilitate the perpetration of child sexual abuse, impede detection of abuse, and undermine response to abuse occurring in organizational contexts. In this Element we briefly outlined the implications of our analysis for practitioners devoted to protecting children from sexual abuse and the apprehending and prosecuting abusers in organizations, and for organization theorists devoted to the expansion of knowledge about organizations. We hope this Element provides a foundation upon which academics wishing to better understanding child sexual abuse in organizational contexts and practitioners hoping to more effectively curb, uncover, and respond to abuse in these contexts can build to advance knowledge and improve policy in this important domain.

Appendix I

Royal Commission Case Studies Referenced in This Element

(1) *Report of Case Study No. 2: YMCA NSW's response to the conduct of Jonathan Lord.*

(2) *Report of Case Study No. 7: Child sexual abuse at the Parramatta Training School for Girls and the Institution for Girls in Hay.*

(3) *Report of Case Study No. 9: The responses of the Catholic Archdiocese of Adelaide, and the South Australian Police, to allegations of child sexual abuse at St Ann's Special School.*

(4) *Report of Case Study No. 14: The response of the Catholic Diocese of Wollongong to allegations of child sexual abuse, and related criminal proceedings, against John Gerard Nestor, a priest of the Diocese.*

(5) *Report of Case Study No. 15: Response of swimming institutions, the Queensland and NSW Offices of the DPP and the Queensland Commission for Children and Young People and Child Guardian to allegations of child sexual abuse by swimming coaches.*

(6) *Report of Case Study No. 30: The response of Turana, Winlaton and Baltara, Victoria Police and the Department of Health and Human Services Victoria to allegations of child sexual abuse.*

(7) *Transcripts from Case Study No. 32: Geelong Grammar School.*

References

Alicke, M. D. and Sedikides, C. 2011. *Handbook of Self-Enhancement and Self-Protection.* New York, NY: Guilford Press.

Andersen, H. S., D. D. Sestoft, T. T. Lillebæk, G. G. Gabrielsen, R. R. Hemmingsen, and P. P. Kramp. 2000. "A Longitudinal Study of Prisoners on Remand: Psychiatric Prevalence, Incidence and Psycho-Pathology in Solitary vs. Non-Solitary Confinement." *Acta Psychiatrica Scandinavica* 102(1):19.

Archdiocese of Boston. 2002. "Sex-Abuse Scandals Give Rise to Distorted Attacks." New York, USA.

Ashforth, B. E. and V. Anand. 2003. "The Normalization of Corruption in Organizations." *Research in Organizational Behavior* 25:1–52.

Ashforth, B. E., V. Anand, and M. Joshi. 2004. "Business as Usual: The Acceptance and Perpetuation of Corruption in Organizations." *Academy of Management Executive* 18(2):39–53.

Associated Press. 2016. "Oakland Loses 3rd Police Chief amid Growing Scandals." in *The Washington Post.* Washington, DC: The Washington Post.

Auriol, E. and S. Brilon. 2014. "Anti-Social Behavior in Profit and Nonprofit Organizations." *Journal of Public Economics* 117:149–61. doi:10.1016/j. jpubeco.2014.05.006.

Balingit, M. 2017. "Convicted Sex Offender Posed as D.C. School Employee, Drove School Bus for a Week." in *The Washington Post.* Washington, DC: The Washington Post.

Bandura, Albert. 1963. *Social Learning and Personality Development.* New York, NY: Holt, Rinehart, and Winston.

Bartunek, Jean M. 2006. "The Sexual Abuse Scandal as a Social Drama." Pp. 17–30 in *Church Ethics and Its Organizational Context,* edited by J. M. Bartunek, M. A. Hinsdale and J. F. Kennan. Oxford: Rowman and Littlefield Publishers.

Bauman, Zygmunt. 2001. *Modernity and the Holocaust.* Ithaca, NY: Cornell University Press.

Bazerman, M.H. and A. E. Tenbrunsel. 2011. *Blind Spots: Why We Fail to Do What's Right and What to Do about It.* Princeton, NJ: Princeton University Press.

Beck, A. J., P. M. Harrison, and P. Guerino. 2010. "Sexual Victimization in Juvenile Facilities Reported by Youth, 2008–09." Vol. NCJ Report No. 228416.

Bennhold, Katrin. 2016. "Child Sexual Abuse Scandal Rocks U.K. Soccer." in *The New York Times*. New York, NY: The New York Times.

Berry, J. 1992. *Lead Us Not into Temptation: Catholic Priests and the Sexual Abuse of Children*. New York: NY: Doubleday.

Bidgood, Jess. 2015. "In Girl's Account, Ritual at Saint Paul's Boarding School Turned into Rape." in *The New York Times*.

Bilefsky, Dan. 2016. "Jimmy Savile Inquiry Accuses BBC of Failing to Report Sexual Abuse." in *The New York Times*. New York, NY: The New York Times.

Bonesteel, Matt. 2017. "Mckayla Maroney Says USA Gymnastics Team Doctor Began Molesting Her at the Age of 13." in *The Washington Post*. Washington, DC: The Washington Post.

Boorstein, M. and J. Zauzmer. 2016. "'Payout Chart' for Molestation: Secret Archive Held Chilling Details of Clergy Abuse." in *The Washington Post*.

Boston_Globe. 2002. *Betrayal*. Boston, MA: Little, Brown and Company.

Bouffard, J. 2000. "Predicting Type of Sexual Assault Case Closure from Victim, Suspect, and Case Characteristics." *Journal of Criminal Justice* 28: 527–42.

Boulding, K. E. 1958. "Evidences for an Administrative Science: A Review of the *Administrative Science Quarterly*, Volumes 1 and 2." *Administrative Science Quarterly* 3(1):1–22.

Boyle, Patrick. 1994. *Scouts Honor*. Rocklin, CA: Prima Publishing.

Brackenridge, Celia and Sandra L. Kirby. 1997. "Playing Safe: Assessing the Risk of Sexual Abuse to Elite Child Athletes." *International Review for the Sociology of Sport* 32(4):407–18.

Brief, A.P., R.T. Bertram and J. M. Dukerich. 2001. "Collective Corruption in the Corporate World: Toward a Process Model." Pp. 471–99 in *Groups at Work: Advances in Theory and Research*, edited by M. E. Turner. Hillsdale, NJ: Lawrence Erlbaum and Associates.

Bromfield, L. M. 2005. "Chronic Child Maltreatment in an Australian Statutory Child Protection Sample." Deakin University, Geelong. Unpublished Dissertation.

Bromfield, L. M., C. Hirte, O. Octoman and I. Katz. 2017. "Child Sexual Abuse in Australian Institutional Contexts 2008–2013: Findings from Administrative Data." Vol. Sydney, Australia: Royal Commission into Institutional Responses to Child Sexual Abuse.

Burns, John, F. and Alan Cowell. 2013. "Report Depicts Horrific Pattern of Child Sexual Abuse by BBC Celebrity." in *The New York Times*. New York, NY: The New York Times.

Butler, J. 1993. *Bodies that Matter: On the Discursive Limits of "Sex."* London and New York, NY: Routledge.

Cashmore, J. and R. Shackel. 2013. "The Long-Term Effects of Child Sexual Abuse." Sydney, Australia: Child Family Community Australia.

Cashmore, J., A. Taylor, R. Shackel and P. Parkinson. 2016. "The Impact of Delayed Reporting on the Prosecution and Outcomes of Child Sexual Abuse Cases." Sydney, Australia: Royal Commission into Institutional Responses to Child Sexual Abuse. Available at www.childabuseroyalcommission.gov .au/getattachment/e3312f1c-d58f-490d-a467-221684c050c9/The-impact-of-delayed-reporting-on-the-prosecution

CDC. 2012 "Violence against Children in Kenya: Findings from a 2010 National Survey. Summary Report on the Prevalence of Sexual, Physical and Emotional Violence, Context of Sexual Violence, and Health and Behavioral Consequences of Violence Experienced in Childhood." Nairobi, Kenya: United Nations' Children's Fund Kenya Country Office, Division of Violence Prevention, National Center for Injury Prevention and Control, U.S. Centers for Disease Control and Prevention, and the Kenya National Bureau of Statistics.

Cense, M. and C. Brackenridge. 2001. "Temporal and Development Risk Factors for Sexual Harassment and Abuse in Sport." *European Physical Education Review* 7(1):61–79.

Clark, Burton. 1970. *The Distinctive College: Antioch, Reed and Swarthmore.* Chicago, IL: Aldine Publishing Company.

Clarke, R.V. 2008 "Situational Crime Prevention." Pp. 178–94 in *Environmental Criminology and Crime Analysis*, edited by R. Wortley and L. Mazerolle. Cullompton, UK: Willan Publishing.

Coates, G. 1997. "Leadership and Authority: Power, Charisma and Institutional Abuse." *Early Child Development and Care* 133:5–19.

Colton, M., S. Roberts, and M. Vanstone. 2010. "Sexual Abuse by Men Who Work with Children." *Journal of Child Sexual Abuse* 19(3):345–64. doi:10.1080/10538711003775824.

Conte, J., S. Wolf, and T. Smith. 1989a. "What Sexual Offenders Tell Us About Prevention Strategies." *Child Abuse & Neglect* 13:293–301.

Conte, Jon R., Steven Wolf, and Tim Smith. 1989b. "What Sexual Offenders Tell Us About Prevention Strategies." *Child Abuse and Neglect* 13 (2):293–301.

Cutajar, Margaret C., Paul E. Mullen, James R. P. Ogloff, Stuart D. Thomas, David L. Wells, and Josie Spataro. 2010. "Psychopathology in a Large Cohort of Sexually Abused Children Followed up to 43 Years." *Child*

Abuse & Neglect 34(11):813–22. doi:http://dx.doi.org/10.1016/j.chiabu .2010.04.004.

D'Arcy, Mark and Paul Gosling. 1998. *Abuse of Trust: Frank Beck and the Leicestershire Children's Homes Scandal.* London, UK: Bowerdean Publishing Co.

Davis, Gerald, F. and Christopher Marquis. 2005. "Prospects for Organization Theory in the Early Twenty-First Century: Institutional Fields and Mechanisms." *Organization Science* 16(4):332–43.

Davis, Gerald, F. 2006. "Mechanisms and the Theory of Organizations." *Journal of Management Inquiry* 15(2):114–18.

De Freytas-Tamura, Kimiko. 2016. "Draft of Inquiry Report on Jimmy Savile Cites Flaws in BBC Culture." in *The New York Times*. New York, NY: The New York Times.

de la Chaux, Marlen, Helen Haugh, and Royston Greenwood. 2017. "Why Do Lions Lie Down with Wildebeast? Organizing Refugee Camps." edited by University of Cambridge: Cambridge, UK.

de Young, Mary. 2004. *The Day Care Ritual Abuse Moral Panic.* Jefferson, NC: McFarand & Company.

de Young, Mary. 1988. "The Indignant Page: Techniques of Neutralization in the Publications of Pedophile Organizations." *Child Abuse and Neglect* 12 (4):583–91.

DiMaggio, P. J. and W. W. Powell. 1983. "The Iron Cage Revisited: Institutional Isomorphism and Collective Rationality in Organizational Fields." *American Sociological Review* 48(2):147–60.

Dornbush, Sanford M. 1955. "The Military Academy as an Assimilating Institution." *Social Forces* 33(4):316–21.

Elliot, M., K. D. Browne, and J. Kilcoyne. 1995. "Child Sexual Abuse Prevention: What Offenders Tell Us." *Child Abuse & Neglect* 19:579–94.

Erooga, M., D. Allnock, and P. Telford. 2012. "Sexual Abuse of Children by People in Organizations: What Offenders Can Teach Us About Protection." Pp. 63–83 in *Creating Safer Organizations: Practical Steps to Prevent the Abuse of Children by Those Working with Them*, edited by M. Erooga. Chichester, UK: Wiley-Blackwell.

Euser, S., L. R. A. Alink, A. Tharner, M. H. van Ijzendoorn, and M. J. Bakermans-Kranenburg. 2013. "The Prevalence of Child Sexual Abuse in out-of-Home Care: A Comparison between Abuse in Residential and in Foster Care." *Child Maltreatment* 18(4):221–31. doi:10.1177/ 1077559513489848.

Evans, Tim, Mark Alesia, and Marisa Kwiatkowski. 2016. "A 20-Year Toll: 368 Gymnasts Allege Sexual Exploitation." in *IndyStar*. Indianapolis, IN: Gannett Company.

Feiring, C., V. A. Simon, and C. M. Cleland. 2009. "Childhood Sexual Abuse, Stigmatization, Internalizing Symptoms, and the Development of Sexual Difficulties and Dating Aggression." *Journal of Consulting and Clinical Psychology* 77(1):127–37. doi:10.1037/a0013475.

Fergusson, David M., L. John Horwood, and Michael T. Lynskey. 1997. "Childhood Sexual Abuse, Adolescent Sexual Behaviors and Sexual Revictimization." *Child Abuse and Neglect* 21(8):789–803.

Festinger, L. A. 1954. "A Theory of Social Comparison Processes." *Human Relations* 7(2):117–40. doi:10.1177/001872675400700202.

Filipovic, Jill. 2013. "Rape Is About Power, Not Sex." in *The Guardian*. Manchester, UK: The Guardian.

Finkelhor, D., Linda Meyer Williams, and Nanci Burns. 1988. *Nursery Crimes*. Newbury Park, CA: Sage Publications.

Finkelhor, D., Ormrod, R. K., and Turner, H. A. 2007. "Polyvictimization and Trauma in a National Longitudinal Cohort." *Development and Psychopathology* 19(1):149–66. doi:10.1017/S0954579407070083.

Finkelhor, David 1984. *Child Sexual Abuse: New Theory & Research*. New York: Free Press.

Formicola, J. R. 2016. "The Politics of Clerical Sexual Abuse." *Religions* 7(1): 9.

Foucault, M. 1976. *The History of Sexuality: An Introduction*. Translated by R. Hurley. London: Penguin.

French, J.R.P. and B. H. Raven. 1959. "The Bases of Social Power." Pp. 150–67 in *Studies in Social Power*, edited by D. Cartwright. Ann Arbor, MI: Institute for Social Research.

Gerdes, Karen E., Martha N. Beck, Sylvia Cowan-Hancock, and Tracey Wilkinson-Sparks. 1996. "Adult Survivors of Childhood Sexual Abuse: The Case of Mormon Women." *Affilia* 11(1):39–60.

Gibbons-Neff, Thomas. 2015. "Troops Detail Orders to Ignore Sexual Abuse in Afghanistan, Despite General's Denial." in *The Washington Post*.

Giorgi, S., C. Lockwood, and M. A. Glynn. 2015. "The Many Faces of Culture: Making Sense of 30 Years of Research on Culture in Organizational Studies." *The Academy of Management Annals* 9(1):1–54.

Goffman, Erving. 1961. "On the Characteristics of Total Institutions." Pp. 1–124 in *Asylums*. New York: Anchor Books.

Goldenberg, Rachel. 2013. "Unholy Clergy: Amending State Child Abuse Reporting Statutes to Include Clergy Members as Mandatory Reporters in

Child Sexual Abuse Cases." *Family Court Review* 51(2):298–315. doi:http://dx.doi.org/10.1111/fcre.12028.

Goldstein, Joseph. 2015. "U.S. Soldiers Told to Ignore Sexual Abuse of Boys by Afghan Allies." in *The New York Times*. New York, NY: The New York Times Company.

Goldsworthy, Kathryn. 2015. "What Is Child Abuse and Neglect." Vol.: Australian Institute of Family Studies.

Goleman, Daniel. 1991. "Sexual Harassment: It's About Power, Not Lust." in *The New York Times*. New York, NY: The New York Times.

Green, L. and H. Masson. 2002. "Adolescents Who Sexually Abuse and Residential Accommodation: Issues of Risk and Vulnerability." *British Journal of Social Work* 32:149–68.

Green, Lorraine. 2001. "Analysing the Sexual Abuse of Children by Workers in Residential Care Homes: Characteristics, Dynamics and Contributory Factors." *Journal of Sexual Aggression* 7(2):5–24. doi:http://dx.doi.org/10.1080/13552600108416164.

Grosz, E. 1995. *Space, Time, and Perversion: Essays on the Politics of Bodies*. New York and London: Routledge.

Hancock, Adrienne B. and Benjamin A. Rubin. 2014. "Influence of Communication Partner's Gender on Language." *Journal of Language and Social Psychology* 34(1):46–64.

Haney, C., W. C. Banks, and P. G. Zimbardo. 1973. "Interpersonal Dynamics in a Simulated Prison." *International Journal of Criminology and Penology* 1:69–97.

Hanson, R. Karl, Andrew J. R. Harris, Elizabeth Letourneau, L. Maaike Helmus, and David Thornton. 2018. "Reductions in Risk Based on Time Offense Free in the Community: Once a Sexual Offender, Not Always a Sexual Offender." *Psychology, Public Policy, and Law* 24(1): 48–63.

Hartill, M. 2005. "Sport and the Sexually Abused Male Child." *Sport Education and Society* 10(3):287–304. doi:10.1080/13573320500254869.

Hartill, M. 2013. "Concealment of Child Sexual Abuse in Sports." *Quest* 65(2): 241–54. doi:10.1080/00336297.2013.773532.

Hartill, Mike. 2009. "The Sexual Abuse of Boys in Organized Male Sports." *Men and Masculinities* 12(2):225–49. doi:http://dx.doi.org/10.1177/1097184X07313361.

Herman, Judith. 2015 *Trauma and Recovery: The Aftermath of Violence–from Domestic Abuse to Political Terror*. NY: Basic Books.

Hersh, Seymore, M. 2004a. "Torture at Abu Ghraib." *The New Yorker*, May 10.

Hersh, Seymore, M. 2004b. "Chain of Command: How the Department of Defense Mishandled the Disaster at Abu Ghraib." *The New Yorker*, May 17.

Hinings, C. R. and R. Greenwood. 2002. "Disconnects and Consequences in Organization Theory?." *Administrative Science Quarterly* 47:411–21.

Hinings, C. R. and Michael K. Mauws. 2006. "Organizational Morality." Pp. 115–22 in *Church Ethics and Its Organizational Context*, edited by J. M. Bartunek, M. A. Hinsdale and J. F. Kennan. Oxford, UK: Rowman and Littlefield Publishers.

Hobson, W. 2017. "Doctor at Center of USA Gymnastics Scandal Left Warning Signs at Michigan State." in *The Washington Post*. Washington, DC: The Washington Post.

Hobson, Will and Steven Rich. 2017. "Every Six Weeks for More Than 36 Years: When Will Sex Abuse in Olympic Sports End?" in *The Washington Post*. Washington, DC: The Washington Post.

Humphreys, C. 1992. "Disclosure of Child Sexual Assault: Implications for Mothers. Australian Social Work." 45(3):27–36. doi:10.1080/03124079208550152.

Irenyi, M., L. Bromfield, L. Beyer, and D. Higgins. 2006. "Child Maltreatment in Organizations: Risk Factors and Strategies for Prevention." Vol. 25. *National Child Protection Clearinghouse Issues*. Melbourne: Australian Institute of Family Studies.

Jackall, R. 1988. *Moral Mazes*. Oxford, UK: Oxford University Press.

Jones, Jonathan. 2012. "Freeh Report: Two Janitors Saw Sandusky Abuse but Feared for Jobs." *Sports Illustrated*, July 12.

Kamil, Amos. 2012. "Prep-School Predators: The Horace Mann School's Secret History of Sexual Abuse." in *The New York Times Magazine*. New York, NY.

Kaufman, Keith and M. Erooga. 2016. "Risk Profiles for Institutional Child Sexual Abuse: A Literature Review." Sydney, Australia: Royal Commission into Institutional Responses to Child Sexual Abuse.

Kay, Katty. 2002. "Us Media "Hounding" Vatican over Sex." in *London Times*. London, UK.

Keenan, Marie. 2012. *Child Sexual Abuse and the Catholic Church: Gender, Power, and Organizational Culture*. Oxford, UK: Oxford University Press.

Keltner, D., D. H. Gruenfeld, and C. Anderson. 2003. "Power, Approach, and Inhibition." *Psychological Review* 110:265–84.

Kilpatrick, D. G., H. S. Resnick, K. J. Ruggiero, L. M. Conoscenti and J. McCauley. 2007. "Drug-Facilitated, Incapacitated, and Forcible Rape: A National Study." Washington, DC: National Institute of Justice.

Kipnis, David. 1972. "Does Power Corrupt?." *Journal of Personality and Social Psychology* Vol 24:33–41.

Knopf, T. A. 2016. "Where Were Boston's TV Stations During the Church Sex Abuse Scandal?" *Columbia Journalism Review.*

Krakauer, J. 2015. *Missoula: Rape and the Justice System in a College Town.* New York, NY: Anchor Books.

LaCanna, X. 2015. "Sex Abuse and Violence: Secrets of Retta Dixon Home for Aboriginal Children Laid Bare at Royal Commission." in *Australian Broadcasting Corporation.*

Lanning, Kenneth V. and Park Dietz. 2014. "Acquaintance Molestation and Youth-Serving Organizations." *Journal of Interpersonal Violence* 29(15): 2815–38.

Lee-Chai, A. Y., S. Chen and T. L. Chartrand. 2001. "From Moses to Marcos: Individual Differences in the Use and Abuse of Power." Pp. 57–74 in *The Use and Abuse of Power,* edited by A. Y. Lee-Chai and J. A. Bargh. Philadelphia, PA: Psychology Press.

Letourneau, E., William Eaton, Judity Bass, S. Berlin Frederick and Steven G. Moore. 2014. "The Need for a Comprehensive Public Health Approach to Preventing Child Sexual Abuse." *Public Health Reports* 129(May–June): 222–28.

Letourneau, E. 2016. "Child Sexual Abuse Is Preventable, Not Inevitable." TEDMED. (http://tedmed.com/talks/show?id=620399).

Lindblad, F., P. Gustafsson, I. Larsson, and B. Lundin. 1995. "Preschoolers' Sexual Behaviour at Day Care Centers: An Epidemiological Study." *Child Abuse & Neglect* 19:569–77.

Lindert, J., O. S. Ehrenstein, R. Grashow, G. Gal, E. Braehler, and M. G. Weisskopf. 2013. "Sexual and Physical Abuse in Childhood Is Associated with Depression and Anxiety over the Life Course: Systematic Review and Meta-Analysis." *International Journal of Public Health* 59(2):359–72. doi:1007/s00038-013–0519-5.

Lisak, D., L. Gardinier, S. C. Nicksa, and A. M. Cole. 2010. "False Allegations of Sexual Assault: An Analysis of Ten Years of Reported Cases." *Violence against Women* 16(12).

Lonsway, K. A. and J. Archambault. 2012. "The 'Justice Gap' for Sexual Assault Cases: Future Directions for Research and Reform." *Violence against Women* 18(2): 145-168.

March, J. G. and H. Simon. 1958. *Organizations.* New York, NY: John Wiley & Sons.

Mckenzie-Murray, Martin. 2015. "Hiding Sexual Abuse Behind Prestige at Geelong Grammar." *The Saturday Paper,* September 12.

McKibbin, G., Humphreys, C., and Hamilton, B. 2015. "Prevention-Enhancing Interactions: A Critical Interpretive Synthesis of the Evidence About

Children Who Sexually Abuse Other Children." *Health & Social Care in the Community*. doi:10.1111/hsc.12260.

Mechanic, D. 1962. "Sources of Power of Lower Participants in Complex Organizations." *Administrative Science Quarterly* 7:349–64.

Mendel, Matthew Parynik. 1995. *The Male Survivor: The Impact of Sexual Abuse*. Thousand Oaks, CA: Sage Publications, Inc.

Menzies, K. and L. Stoker. 2015. "When 'Culture Trumped Safety,' Developing a Protective Weave in Child Welfare Organisations: A Case Study." *Children Australia* 40(3):260–68. doi:10.1017/cha.2015.22.

Mettler, Katie. 2016. "Texas Teacher Had Sex with Her 8th Grade English Student 'on Almost a Daily Basis,' Police Say." in *The Washington Post*. Washington, DC.

Meyer, J. W. and B. Rowan. 1977. "Institutionalized Organizations: Formal Structure as Myth and Ceremony." *American Journal of Sociology* 83: 340–63.

Middleton, Warwick, Pam Stavropoulos, Martin J. Dorahy, Christa Krüger, Roberto Lewis-Fernández, Alfonso Martínez-Taboas, Vedat Sar, and Bethany Brand. 2014. "The Australian Royal Commission into Institutional Responses of Child Sexual Abuse." *Australian and New Zealand Journal of Psychiatry* 48(1):17–21. doi:http://dx.doi.org/10.1177/0004867413514639.

Milgram, Stanley. 1974. *Obedience to Authority*. New York, NY: Harper and Row.

Mintz, B. and Schwartz, M. 1985 *Bank Hegemony*. Chicago, IL: University of Chicago Press.

Moch, Michael and Anne S. Huff. 1983. "Power Enactment through Language and Ritual." *Journal of Business Research* 11:293–316.

Mones, Paul. 2014. "Response to 'Acquaintance Molestation and Youth-Serving Organizations' by Kenneth V. Lanning and Park Dietz." *Journal of Interpersonal Violence* 29(15):2855–58. doi:http://dx.doi.org/10.1177/0886260514532363.

Moore, D.A., P. E. Tetlock, L. Tanlu, and M. H. Bazerman.2006. "Conflicts of Interest and the Case of Auditor Independence: Moral Seduction and Strategic Issue Cycling." *Academy of Management Review* 31(1):10–29.

Moulden, H. M., P. Firestone, D. A. Kingston, and A. F. Wexler. 2010. "A Description of Sexual Offending Committed by Canadian Teachers." *Journal of Child Sexual Abuse* 19(4):403–18. doi:10.1080/10538712.2010.495046.

Nadler, D. A. and E. E. Lawler. 1977. "Motivation: A Diagnostic Approach." Pp. 25–36 in *Psychological Dimensions of Organizational Behavior* edited by B. M. Staw. Upper Saddle River, NJ: Pearson Education.

Neustein, Amy and Michael Lesher. 2008. "A Single-Case Study of Rabbinic Sexual Abuse in the Orthodox Jewish Community." *Journal of Child Sexual Abuse* 17(3–4):270–89.

Nielsen, Richard. 2018. "Who Do We Identify With: Ontological and Epistemological Challenges of Spanning Different Domains of Academic-Practitioner Praxis." in *Academic–Practitioner Relationships: Developments, Complexities and Opportunities*, edited by J. M. Bartunek and J. McKenzie. New York, NY: Routledge.

Ogloff, J., M. Cutajar, Eberhard M. Mann, and P. Mullen. 2012. "Child Sexual Abuse and Subsequent Offending and Victimization: A 45 Year Follow-up Study." Vol. ISSN 1836–2206. Canberra, Australia: Australian Institute of Criminology.

Palmer, D., V. Feldman, and G. McKibbin. 2016. "The Role of Culture in Child Sexual Abuse in Institutional Contexts." Vol.: Royal Commission into Institutional Responses to Child Sexual Abuse.

Palmer, D. 2008. "Extending the Process Model of Collective Organizational Wrongdoing." *Research in Organizational Behavior* 28:107–35.

Palmer, Donald. 2012. *Normal Organizational Wrongdoing: A Critical Analysis of Theories of Misconduct in and by Organizations*. Oxford, UK: Oxford University Press.

Palmer, Donald. 2017. "Institutions, Institutional Theory, and Organizational Wrongdoing." Pp. 737–758 in *Sage Handbook of Organizational Institutionalism*, edited by R. Greenwood, C. Oliver, T. B. Lawrence, and R. E. Meyer. London, UK: Sage.

Palmer, Donald and Valerie Feldman. 2017. "Toward a More Comprehensive Analysis of the Role of Organizational Culture in Child Sexual Abuse in Institutional Contexts." *Child Abuse & Neglect*, 74:23–34.

Palmer, Donald, Nicole Biggart, and Brian Dick. 2008. "Is the New Institutionalism a Theory?" Pp. 739–68 in *The Sage Handbook of Organizational Institutionalism*, edited by R. Greenwood, C. Oliver, R. Suddaby, and K. Sahlin-Anderson. London, UK: Sage Publications.

Paolucci, E. O., M.L. Genuis, and C. Violato. 2001. "A Meta-Analysis of the Published Research on the Effects of Child Sexual Abuse." *The Journal of Psychology* 135(1):17–36. doi:10.1080/00223980109603677.

Parent, Sylvie. 2011. "Disclosure of Sexual Abuse in Sport Organizations: A Case Study." *Journal of Child Sexual Abuse* 20(3):322–37. doi:http://dx.doi.org/10.1080/10538712.2011.573459.

Parent, Sylvie and Guylaine Demers. 2011. "Sexual Abuse in Sport: A Model to Prevent and Protect Athletes." *Child Abuse Review* 20(2):120–33. doi: http://dx.doi.org/10.1002/car.1135.

Parent, Sylvie and Joelle Bannon. 2012. "Sexual Abuse in Sport: What About Boys?" *Children and Youth Services Review* 34(2):354–59. doi:http://dx.doi .org/10.1016/j.childyouth.2011.11.004.

Parkin, Wendy and Lorraine Green. 1997. "Cultures of Abuse within Residential Child Care." *Early Child Development and Care* 133: 73–8.

Parsons, Talcott. 1956a. "Suggestions for a Sociological Approach to the Theory of Organizations. I." *Administrative Science Quarterly* 1: 63–85.

Parsons, Talcott. 1956b. "Suggestions for a Sociological Approach to the Theory of Organizations. Ii." *Administrative Science Quarterly* 1:225–39.

Patterson, D. and R. Campbell. 2010. "Why Rape Survivors Participate in the Criminal Justice System." *Journal of Community Psychology* 38(2):191–205.

Pereda, Noemí, Georgina Guilera, Maria Forns, and Juana Gómez-Benito. 2009. "The Prevalence of Child Sexual Abuse in Community and Student Samples: A Meta-Analysis." *Clinical Psychology Review* 29(4):328–38. doi: http://dx.doi.org/10.1016/j.cpr.2009.02.007.

Perrow, Charles. 2014. *Complex Organizations: A Critical Essay*. Brattleboro, VT: Echo Point Books & Media.

Perrucci, R. and Pilisuk, M. 1970. "Leaders and Ruling Elites: The Interorganizational Basis of Community Power." *American Sociological Review* 36:1040–57.

Pfeffer, J. and G. R. Salancik. 1978. *The External Control of Organizations*. New York, NY: Harper and Row.

Pfeffer, J. 1981. *Power in Organizations*. London, UK: Pitman Publishing Corporation.

Pfeffer, J. 2016. "Why the Assholes Are Winning: Money Trumps All." *Journal of Management Inquiry* 54(4):663–69.

Pfeffer, J. and A. Davis-Blake. 1989. "Just a Mirage: The Search for Dispositional Effects in Organizational Research" *Academy of Management Review* 14(3):385–400.

Pfeffer, Jeffrey. 1976. "Beyond Management and the Worker: The Institutional Function of Management." *The Academy of Management Review* 1 (2):36–46.

Powell, A. 2008. "Amor Fati?: Gender Habitus and Young People's Negotiation of (Hetero)Sexual Consent." *Journal of Sociology* 44(2):167–84.

Price-Robertson, Rhys, Leah Bromfield and Suzanne Vassallo. 2010. *"The Prevalence of Child Abuse and Neglect."* Vol. Melbourne.

Pringle, Keith. 1993. "Child Sexual Abuse Perpetrated by Welfare Personnel and the Problem of Men." *Critical Social Policy* 12:4–19.

Rice, P. 2002. "Gregory Hails People's Response to Us Scandal: 'He Gets It'." Pp. B1 in *St. Louis Post-Dispatch*. Saint Louis: Mo.

Richards, Kelly. 2011. "Misperceptions About Child Sex Offenders." Vol. *Trends and Issues in Crime and Criminal Justice*. Australian Institute of Criminology.

Rogers, E. M. 2003. *Diffusion of Innovation*. New York: Free Press.

Royal_Commission_into_Institutional_Responses_to_Child_Sexual_Abuse. 2015. "Request for Tender: The Role of Organizational Culture in Child Sexual Abuse in Institutional Contexts." Vol.

Rubin, M. and Hewstone, M. 1998. "Social Identity Theory's Selfesteem Hypothesis: A Review and Some Suggestions for Clarification." *Personality and Social Psychology Review* 2:40–62.

Ruhl, J. and D. Ruhl. 2015. "NCR Research: Costs of Sex Abuse Crisis to Us Church Underestimated." in *National Catholic Reporter*. Kansas City, MO: National Catholic Reporter Publishing Company.

Schein, E. H. 1985. *Organizational Culture and Leadership*. San Francisco, CA: Jossey-Bass Publishers.

Schein, E. H. 1995. "The Role of the Founder in Creating Organizational Culture." *Family Business Review* 8(3):221–38.

Schewe, Paul A. and William O'Donohue. 1996. "Rape Prevention with High-Risk Males: Short-Term Outcome of Two Interventions." *Archives of Sexual Behavior* 25(5):455–71.

Schumacher, Ruth B. and Rebecca S. Carlson. 1999. "Variables and Risk Factors Associated with Child Abuse in Daycare Settings." *Child Abuse and Neglect* 23(9):891–98.

Scott, S. 2010. "Revisiting the Total Institution: Performative Regulation in the Reinventive Institution." *Sociology* 44(2):213–31.

Scott, W. Richard. 2008. "Approaching Adulthood: The Maturing of Institutional Theory." *Theory and Society* 37(5):427–42.

Scott, W. Richard. 1987. "The Adolescence of Institutional Theory." *Administrative Science Quarterly* 32:493–511.

Selznick, Philip. 1948. "Foundations of a Theory of Organizations." *American Sociological Review* 13:25–35.

Selznick, Philip. 1949. *TVA and the Grass Roots*. Berkeley and Los Angeles, USA: University of California Press.

Shakeshaft, C. and A. Cohan. 1994. "In Loco Parentis: Sexual Abuse of Students in Schools (What Administrators Should Know)." *Administration and Policy Studies* Hofstra University. (January): 1–40.

Shakeshaft, Charol. 2004. *Educator Sexual Misconduct: A Synthesis of Existing Literature PPSS 2004-09* Congress.

Shakeshaft, Charol. 2014. "Response to "Acquaintance Molestation and Youth-Serving Organizations" by Kenneth V. Lanning and Park Dietz." *Journal of Interpersonal Violence* 29(15):2849–54.

Shils, Edward and Henry A. Finch. 2011. *Methodology of the Social Sciences.* Piscataway, NJ: Transaction Publishers.

Simon, R. I. 1995. "The Natural History of Therapist Sexual Misconduct: Identification and Prevention." *Psychiatric Annals* 25:90–94.

Smallbone, Stephen, William L. Marshall, and Richard Wortley. 2008. *Preventing Child Sexual Abuse: Evidence, Policy and Practice.* Devon: Willan Publishing.

Smith, Andrea. 2004. "Boarding School Abuses, Human Rights, and Reparations." *Social Justice* 31(4):89–102.

Spohn, C., D. Beichner, and E. Davids-Frenzel. 2001. "Prosecutorial Justifications for Sexual Assault Case Rejection: Guarding the 'Gateway to Justice'." *Social Problems* 48:206–35.

Sprober, N., T. Schneider, M. Rassenhofer, A. Seitz, H. Liebhardt, L. Konig, and J. M. Fegert. 2014. "Child Sexual Abuse in Religiously Affiliated and Secular Institutions: A Retrospective Descriptive Analysis of Data Provided by Victims in a Government-Sponsored Reappraisal Program in Germany." *BMC Public Health* 14. doi:10.1186/1471–2458-14–282.

St. George, Donna. 2017. "Nearly 850 Employees in Md. School System on Leave This Year as Child Abuse Investigations Soar." in *The Washington Post.* Washington, DC: The Washington Post.

Staller, Karen M. 2012. "Missing Pieces, Repetitive Practices: Child Sexual Exploitation and Institutional Settings." *Cultural Studies – Critical Methodologies* 12(4):274–78. doi:http://dx.doi.org/10.1177/1532708612446420.

Staw, B. M. 1976. "Knee-Deep in the Big Muddy: A Study of Escalating Commitment to a Chosen Couse of Action." *Organizational Behavior and Human Performance* 16:27–44.

Staw, B. M. 2016. "Stumbling Towards a Social Psychology of Organizations: An Autobiographical Look at the Changing Nature of Organizational Research." *Annual Review of Organizational Psychology and Organizational Behavior* 3: 1–19.

Stern, R. N. and S. R. Barley. 1996. "Organizations and Social Systems: Organization Theory's Neglected Mandate." *Administrative Science Quarterly* 41:146–62.

Stillman, Sarah. 2016. "The List." *The New Yorker.*

Stokes, Donald E. 1997. *Pasteur's Quadrant: Basic Science and Technological Innovation.* Washington, DC: Brookings Institution Press.

Stoltenborgh, M., M. H. van Ijzendoorn, E. M. Euser, and M. J. Bakermans-Kranenburg. 2011. "A Global Perspective on Child Sexual Abuse: Meta-Analysis of Prevalence around the World." *Child Maltreatment* 16 (2):79–101. doi:10.1177/1077559511403920.

Sykes, G. and D. Matza. 1957. "Techniques of Neutralization: A Theory of Delinquency." *American Sociological Review* 22(6):664–70.

Terry, K. 2015. "Child Sexual Abuse within the Catholic Church: A Review of Global Perspectives." *International Journal of Comparative and Applied Criminal Justice* 39(2):139–54.

Thornton, P. H., W. Ocasio, and M. Lounsbury. 2012. *The Institutional Logics Perspective.* Oxford, UK: Oxford University Press.

Timmerman, Margaretha C. and Pauline R. Schreuder. 2014. "Sexual Abuse of Children and Youth in Residential Care: An International Review." *Aggression and Violent Behavior* 19:715–20.

Tucci, J., J. Mitchell, D. Holmes, C. Hemsworth, and L. Hemsworth. 2015. "Constructing a Child Protection Policy to Support a Safeguarding Children Culture in Organisations and Institutions." *Children Australia* 40(1):78–86. doi:10.1017/cha.2014.42.

Vadera, Abhijeet K. and Michael G. Pratt. 2016. "'Is It Me? Or Is It Me?' the Role of Co-Activated Multiple Identities and Identifications in Promoting or Discouraging Workplace Crimes." in *Organizational Wrongdoing: Key Perspectives and New Directions*, edited by D. Palmer, K. Smith-Crowe and R. Greenwood. Cambridge, UK: Cambridge University Press.

Vatican. 2002. "Final Communique of the Meeting between the Cardinals of the United States and the Pope."

Vaughan, Dianne. 1996. *The Challenger Launch Decision: Risky Technology, Culture, and Deviance at Nasa.* Chicago, IL: University of Chicago Press.

Ward, T. and R. J. Siegert. 2002. "Toward a Comprehensive Theory of Child Sexual Abuse: A Theory Knitting Perspective." *Psychology, Crime & Law* 8 (4):319–51.

Weber, M. 1946. "Class, Status, and Party." in *From Max Weber: Essays in Sociology*, edited by H. H. Gerth and C. W. Mills. Oxford, UK: Oxford University Press.

Weber, M. 2011. *The Protestant Ethic and the Spirit of Capitalism*. Oxford, UK: Oxford University Press.

Webster, R. 1999. "Crusade or Witch-Hunt?" *Times Literary Supplement*, 22 January.

Weick, K. E. and K.H. Roberts. 1993. "Collective Mind in Organizations: Heedful Interrelating on Flight Decks." *Administrative Science Quarterly* 38(3):357–81.

Weinger, M. 2015. "Men Still Dominate Executive Ranks at Big Groups." *Financial Times*, December 29.

Whiffen, V.E. and H. B. Macintosh. 2005. "Mediators of the Link between Childhood Sexual Abuse and Emotional Distress: A Critical Review." *Trauma Violence Abuse* 6(1):24–39.

WHO. 2006. "Preventing Child Maltreatment: A Guide to Taking Action and Generating Evidence" Vol. Geneva, Switzerland: World Health Organisation and International Society for Prevention of Child Abuse and Neglect.

Wilson, M. 2009. "Benchmarking Women's Leadership." Vol. NY: NY: The White House Project.

Wurtle, S. K. 2012. "Preventing the Sexual Exploitation of Minors in Youth-Serving Organizations." *Children and Youth Services Review* 34: 2442–53.

Zald, M. 1969. "The Power and Function of Boards of Directors: A Theoretical Synthesis." *American Journal of Sociology* 75:97–111.

Zauzmer, J. 2016. "In 'Groundbreaking' Case, Franciscan Friars Charges with Allowing Abuse of at Least 80 Kids." in *The Washington Post*.

Zimbardo, P. G. 2010. *The Lucifer Effect: Understanding How Good People Turn Evil*. New York: Random House.

Zimmerman, Don H. and Candice West. 1996. "Sex Roles, Interruptions, and Silences in Conversation." *Amsterdam Studies in the Theory and History of Linguistic Science Series* 4:211–36.

Acknowledgments

The authors are grateful to Jean Bartunek, Erica Palmer, Katie Wright, and the staff of the Australian Royal Commission into Institutional Responses to Child Sexual Abuse for their helpful comments on earlier manifestations of this work. They are also indebted to Nelson Phillips, Royston Greenwood, and Elizabeth J. Latourneau for valuable guidance on earlier versions of this manuscript.

Cambridge Elements ≡

Organization Theory

Nelson Phillips
Imperial College London
Nelson Phillips is the Abu Dhabi Chamber Professor of Strategy and Innovation at Imperial College London. His research interests include organization theory, technology strategy, innovation, and entrepreneurship, often studied from an institutional theory perspective.

Royston Greenwood
University of Alberta
Royston Greenwood is the Telus Professor of Strategic Management at the University of Alberta, a Visiting Professor at the University of Cambridge, and a Visiting Professor at the University of Edinburgh. His research interests include organizational change and professional misconduct.

Advisory Board
Paul Adler *USC*
Mats Alvesson *Lund University*
Steve Barley *University of Santa Barbara*
Jean Bartunek *Boston College*
Paul Hirsch *Northwestern University*
Ann Langley *HEC Montreal*
Renate Meyer *WU Vienna*
Danny Miller *HEC Montreal*
Mike Tushman *Harvard University*
Andrew Van de Ven *University of Minnesota*

About the Series
Organization theory covers many different approaches to understanding organizations, its focus is on what constitutes the how and why of organizations and organizing, bringing understanding of organizations in a holistic way. The purpose of *Elements in Organization Theory* is to systematize and contribute to our understanding of organizations.

Cambridge Elements ≡

Organization Theory

Elements in the Series

Printed in the United States
By Bookmasters